SPIRITUAL
PRACTICALITY

• •

THE SEVEN KEYS TO THE MYSTERIES OF THE
AGELESS WISDOM

Rev. Douglas Fisichella

Ordering Information:

For orders and inquiries, please contact:
1-888-375-9818
www.toplinkpublishing.com
bookorder@toplinkpublishing.com

Printed in the United States of America

CONTENTS

This book is dedicated to Louise Main and to the union I experienced with her during our 22 years together. The effect it has had on my consciousness has been undeniable in good times and difficult ones as well. Without these experiences my life would not have been the fulfilling journey it has been, and without her support of my work it would have been impossible.

ACKNOWLEDGEMENTS

I would like to say thank you, and acknowledge some of the people who have had an enormous contribution to my life and my understanding of the world around me. My brother Tony tops the list. He is my consigliere in hard times and incredibly supportive at all times. My mother, Jeanne Resen helped with editing and has always been an amazing counselor as well. Along with her husband Warren Resen they form the foundation for our family.

I would also like to acknowledge the generosity of my sisters Dori, Jeanne-Marie, and Christine in helping to start and fund Higher Ground and the presentation of my father's work which was a pivotal point in my journey and ultimately, the creation of this book.

My Alice Bailey study group, which has at its core, Betty Maxwell, Janet Jacobs, Linda Rinelli, Margo Yoder, Gary Marx, Fred Van Ackeren, Mary Belle Knudson, Dorene Miller, Jan Earp and Phelan Earp, has been an anchor for me and a source of much food for thought. The same core group Along with Angela and Ahmed Koroosa forms the central force of The Denver Goodwill Service Group who have been meeting and serving humanity for decades. These are my teachers and students, friends and companions, on the lighted way.

The Headquarters Group at the Arcane School of the Lucis Trust which has been a source of gentle guidance and insight through my ten years of study there.

I would also like to thank the members of the Metaphysical Research Society of Denver and specifically Gina Viola, Mary Lovejoy, Monica Lewis and Kathrine Apitz, Elaine Nicholas, Duane Leikens, Amber Olson, John Stirling Walker, Joe Raucci, Richard Kotlarz, and Robert Mazzorana for their guidance and support over the years.

I would like to thank Mark Yarnes for his loyal friendship, Kathy Gann and the Denver Theosophical Society, Pastor Susan Miller and the entire group at First Spiritual Science Church for their love and support as well.

A special thanks also, to Bruce Morrison and Rebecca Bauer for their continuing love and the acceptance and guidance they have given me along this rocky road, and to Michiko Theis whose love and encouragement carried me through difficult times and brought me back to teaching.

And finally I want to thank my father Anthony J. Fisichella and my brother Nick. While they were not here physically, their influence on my life and their constant presence in my heart and mind have undoubtedly guided my work.

FOREWORD

They say the only constant is change. It is also said, that some things never change. Both are true. If we look to science, its history and present advances, we are affirmed that as we discover and understand more, we realize just how much more there is to learn. The more we define, the more we realize the nature of the infinite and the eternal. They seem to reveal each other. With each advance, and each emergence of complexity and expansion, we find threads that endure. The simple laws at the astronomical, atomic and quantum levels are few in number but define, contain and organize all the chaos and beauty we encounter every day. To realize there is freedom and design is an amazing thing. Spiritual Practicality can reveal this for you.

Most of us organize our lives according to what we could call "relative rules." This means that we live by rules and codes and expectations that are not just from our actual relatives and family, but our culture, our time period, our social class, our schooling and all other forms of conditioning. These unspoken rules are also developed in reaction to our own unique experiences - good and not so good. It is not a terrible thing to live by conditioning. A lot of life's stress is just the distance between our expectations and our reality. So, if your choices reflect the support and approval around you, that is not always a mistake.

The trouble with the unspoken rules that most of us follow is that they are usually taught and followed as if they were absolute rules, and as if they were universally true. This is a problem for two reasons. No human rules can be 100% true 100% of the time because they are always interpreted and we haven't encountered every imaginable situation. Not yet. No one is always right. Even ultimate life lessons and values which have an alignment with our Source and the quantum rule, can still be doubted or disagreed with. That is just human nature.

The second, and more significant reason that following our conditioning without question can be problematic, is that we are each born with an innate personality - soul, spirit, self, essences, character, or whatever you want to call it. This inner force is not subjective and will let us know, through emotion and energy, when we are on track or off, authentic or not. Conditioning can make it hard to embrace the truth of who we are, but not embracing ourselves is a dangerous path with many costs.

In a curious and parallel way, it seems that life and the universe itself has its own true nature and its own conditioning. The conditioning is the stories we have made up about life: it is our myths, and cultures and our own ideas. Even science has more limits than certainties. Nevertheless, we have converged on some simple principles that can be tested and tested and tested and seem to continue to prove "true." This is both physically and metaphysically the case. Since the beginning of time people have studied the inner world of human experience and the subtle realms of life, love and energy.

Despite the endless versions of God and "how things work," there appears to be a core set of insights, a persistent wisdom that can be found throughout the ages. When we learn these principles and align our own authentic choices with them an unmistakable magic emerges. We become resilient, hopeful, joyful and linked to a sense of self and purpose that transcends our conditions and conditioning. Of all of life's journeys, this is perhaps the most precious and powerful. Spiritual Practicality is one of those rare books that takes vast and complex knowledge and translates in a clear, organized and accessible way. If you seek to align your life with the same forces that created it, this is a great place to start.

Jonathan Ellerby PhD, bestselling author of Return to the Sacred

INTRODUCTION TO THE ESOTERIC SCIENCES

The phone is ringing. I'm asleep but slowly becoming aware. As I open my eyes the reality of my place in time and space creeps into my consciousness. It's after 3:00 am Monday morning and I'm in a hotel room in Fresno, CA. At that instant I know the reason for the call. My father had passed. The phone also rang when I had first arrived at my hotel three and a half hours earlier. It was my brother Tony and his first words were "guess who is still alive?" Dad was out of surgery and I could go to sleep. Now the phone is ringing again, and I know he is gone.

Over the past twenty-four hours or so, he had gone from a healthy seventy-one year old vegetarian, to spending the night in a hospital for the first time in his life and having surgery on his heart. An aortic aneurism awoke him from his sleep Sunday morning and he needed emergency surgery. When I found out about this, I was already preparing for the business trip that brought me to this unlikely place to experience this loss alone. It would have been impossible for me to fly to Florida to see him before the surgery, so taking my trip was an act of faith. He was going to be fine. He was surrounded by family. Running to Florida felt like it would have been acting on the fear of his death, so in an effort to live my faith, I decided to go to Fresno.

Later Monday morning I had to call my friend and boss Dennis and get him to cover me. He knew nothing of my predicament because I knew that if I had told him, he would have sent me to my family. After tying up some loose ends, he began the drive from San Francisco. This would allow me to head to Florida after one of the longest days I have ever experienced and see a friendly face before I left. Dennis is a good man and he understood why I kept silent, even though it put quite a kink in his world. He acknowledged that he never would have let me take the trip to Fresno but understood why I had to go.

That moment in the middle of the night changed the course of my life and ultimately led to the creation of the book you have in your hand. In a strange way, dad's departure was yet another gift. I felt a responsibility not only to him, but to the world, to bring out his three unpublished books. The trilogy is called "One Solitary Life." Reading and editing them took me deeper into the teaching that guided his life, and now mine, than anything else I have ever experienced. If he were alive, my life would not have taken this beneficent turn. It was starting over and there was a tremendous amount of work to be done - more than I could have imagined. Even though I knew it was up to me to finish his work, I had no idea what the universe had in store for me.

And so it begins...

It might be more appropriate to say it continues, because even a new beginning is a continuation when you are dealing with a succession of cycles. Any process is an uninterrupted stream of change. From the Well of Wisdom lectures my father Anthony J. Fisichella created over forty years ago, a series of cassette tapes were produced. We re-mastered the original recordings rescued by his friend Jules Lynn, and created the CDs released in 2006. Then I revamped and began teaching the course, and now present a book which will follow a similar progression. So, why re-introduce all of this material?

All we effectively are, as you will see, is a self-conscious awareness. An awareness that knows it is aware. In a sense we are really on our way to that knowledge because self-awareness increases as consciousness evolves. All we really have to offer is that awareness or our *attention* and our ability to relate to each other the changes that occur within us as a result of our experiences on the journey of awakening. We hope to do this *in consciousness,* aware of our own nature as we interact and the nature of the universe which constitutes the field of play for our endeavors, as well as their reason and their source.

In writing this book it is my intent to share with you the understanding I have been able to garner through my studies and meditation and to clarify some difficult concepts so that you may define in an informed way what your thoughts, feelings and intuition reveal to you on any one of these supposedly separate subjects. It will help you determine the overall validity of these systems of thought and discipline for yourself.

We will be covering some unfamiliar territory but what I really hope to do is to draw forth from you things that you already know. That is the true meaning of education and it has been my experience with these teachings. They ring a responsive chord in me and I feel I know the truth and knew it before I read it. The Latin root "educare" means to educe or "draw forth from." Unfortunately most educators try to put something in or, *induce.* What we have in the West would be better termed an *inducational* system. I will be positing for your consideration some ideas which may be very new to you on their surface. At the same time, I will be posing questions which will hopefully prompt you to plunge the depths of your intuitive understanding and find your own answers.

Throughout my life, my mother has been my best advisor. As I look back I realize that she rarely answered a question (and she still doesn't). She asked me questions that helped me to clarify my thoughts and my answer would invariably emerge. It has been said that every answer leads to ten more questions and even as scientific knowledge expands, it seems that what they ultimately discover is how little they really know. We will be exploring what are known as the Esoteric Sciences and we will be treating some of the most symbolic and controversial philosophical ideas with a very organized and scientific approach. This is true with the exception that we will be taking on things that science does not permit itself to address.

What do I mean by that? Science is a necessarily restrictive form of investigation that is not allowed to address a question unless it has the possibility of a definitive answer. It is limited by the procedures collectively known as "The Scientific Method" and the rules of the hypothesis.[1] That is simply the nature of the beast. Any attempt to take it in a direction contrary to its methods potentially leads one away from the truth. An example of what can happen is represented by the false theory of the Flying Spaghetti Monster. This is essentially a modern version of Russell's Teapot.[2] It was created as a weapon against the concept known as Intelligent Design, which some are attempting to teach as science in schools. Intelligent Design "theory" basically states that life is too complex to have happened without an intelligent designer or creator. The tongue in cheek counter theory posed by the *Pastafarian* followers of the Spaghetti Monster can be roughly summarized as follows: The universe was created by a deity that looks like spaghetti and meatballs. This creative act was executed in the aftermath of a drinking binge and that is why the universe is imperfect. It sounds ridiculous but is as equally un-provable and, for arguments sake, un-disprovable as any other creationist theory no matter how artistically it is veiled; the real difference being that we have not been taught about (and accepted) the Spaghetti Monster for a couple of thousand years. Nor does its existence make it any easier for our children to deal with grandma's death.

There are five central questions that have occupied man since he truly began to think: Who am I? Where did I come from? What am I doing here? Where am I going? And how do I get there? We are wired to look

---

[1] A hypothesis is a predicted explanation of observed phenomena which, under the scientific method, are based on proven fact and existing laws. In order to be proven they must be subjected to empirical experimental testing. Without a method of proving or falsifying a specific hypothesis it is not recognized by science.

[2] In 1952 Bertrand Russell facetiously proposed the idea of a teapot orbiting the sun that was too small for any telescope to detect. Thus, the inability to detect the teapot could not disprove its existence no matter how powerful the telescope. He reasoned that anyone who believed this would be seen as a fool, but supposed that if it had been taught in ancient books and Sunday Schools, disbelief would constitute eccentricity.

for the meaning that lies behind the events of our lives because we are self-aware.

We see the impact events have in our lives and want to know why things happen. "Why" is a question that is only relative to the inquiring conscious entity but we tend to project reason and reasoning on to another unknown, or un-knowable force, which we imbue with power and wisdom in an effort to give meaning to an occurrence we don't understand. For this reason the majority of our time will be spent looking at a possible model of *how* things all fit together and our functional part in this cosmic dance. The *why* is reserved for you and me to work out for ourselves, through the development of the Higher Intuition.

We will be addressing these issues with logic and reason in our approach but very little I tell you can be proven. This kind of knowledge must be intuited first hand. I will be creating a framework which will give you a basis for your further investigation. I will not ask you to accept anything I say blindly but to simply try to understand what it is I am attempting to get across to you as a cohesive system of thought before you pass judgment on it. I don't believe you should believe anything. I will be your guide and companion through the maze of these complex yet revealing systems of thought, faith and discipline, but the determination of what is truth is left to you.

I am here to give you a black belt in Metaphysics! Now, don't get too excited. What I am intending to do is prepare you for a journey, not start and finish it for you. Anyone who has studied Martial Arts knows that the possessor of a black belt is not really an expert but more of an expert student. This is what I hope to be, as well as what I hope to *bring forth* in you.

The basis and organization of our approach is going to parallel the structure of the Well of Wisdom lectures as my father created them. It represents a progressive look at the field of metaphysics and the esoteric sciences that has been effective for tens of thousands of people. I am glad that I resisted the temptation to re-organize them, because as I have gotten deeper into the teachings this progression has made more sense. Of course I have my own way of understanding and presenting these ideas but in truth none of us own any of this wisdom.

The first thing we need to do is to establish the rules and guidelines that will define our field of inquiry. There have always been pitfalls on the path and we can do ourselves a service by talking about a few of them up front. First, I would like to address the tendency to accept authoritarian teaching. We are programmed to look to authority for guidance when we don't understand something, and many of us take what they say at face value. This is certainly an acceptable approach for certain disciplines but in the case of the spiritual sciences the student is essentially self-taught. While we will always benefit from interaction with other people, the ultimate understanding and assimilation of all knowledge is personal. Adherence to someone else's thought process is foolish at best. If it becomes part of your own understanding because of a resonance within you, then that is a different situation. You are now relying on *your* mind and intuition rather than giving information credibility based on its source.

The Lord Buddha has said; *"We should not believe a thing that is said just because it is said. Nor traditions because they have been handed down from antiquity; nor rumors as such; nor writings by sages because sages wrote them: nor fancies that we may suspect to have been inspired in us by a deva (as in divine spiritual revelation); nor from inferences drawn from some haphazard assumption we may have made; nor because of what seems an analogical necessity; nor on the mere authority of our teachers or masters. But we are to believe when the writing, doctrine or saying is corroborated by our own reason and consciousness."*[3]

What I take from this statement is that the teacher's perspective is not better than yours and it changes every day with experience just like yours does. Truth and actuality differ from reality. Each one of us gets just one perspective through which we can see, experience and

---

[3]   Helena Blavatsky - *The Secret Doctrine: Synthesis of Science, Religion and Philosophy Vol. III.* (London: The Theospohical Publishing Company, 1888)

interact with the world around us but the good news is that we create it ourselves.

Reality is a function of consciousness, and that means it is an interpretation of the world colored by experience. This is by definition a distortion or taint on the information. We not only interpret the world around us but we process the information and project a 3D image of that distorted view back out on the environment before we interact with it.[4] That is why we tend to see what we want to see. We want to listen to an expert and let them do our thinking for us. This is a trap. You will be, in effect, projecting his world view and taking on his reality. It is a great idea to go out and expose yourself to the views of as many people as you care to. Just make up your own mind once you understand what is being presented. This leads to my next point - listening.

Listening is an art and to a certain extent it is a lost art. We tend to live within our own thought processes even when we believe we are listening intently to what is being said. We tend to compare what we are being told with the things we already believe. This sets up an adversarial relationship between what may be a rigid thought form and this new idea. Consequently, it may be ignored because it does not immediately fit into place. When you are being exposed to new information, the key is to avoid the urge to qualify and compare until you have the whole picture. I am going to be using words you know, with meanings you may not assign them. If you are going to understand what I mean you will have to understand what the words mean *to me*. This takes an open mind and heart and some patience. Don't judge, reject, or accept, until you understand. Colonel Henry Steel Olcott, one of the founders of the Theosophical Society, said "We reject nothing without cause and accept nothing without proof." I think that is a wise place to begin.

The start of wisdom is thought to be the acknowledgement that none of us really know what is going on. In Plato's "The Apology," Socrates is told by the Oracle of Delphi that he is a wise man. He does not agree

---

4   Bruce Lipton - *The Biology of Belief: Unleashing the Power of Consciousness, Matter, & Miracles* (Hay House 2005)

with this assessment, which I guess, was the start of his trouble. He sets out across the countryside to find the truth for himself. Everyone he found along the way who claimed to possess wisdom apparently did not. Of a philosopher he met on the road, he said *"Well, although I do not suppose that either of us know anything really beautiful, true, and good, I am better off than he is, for he knows nothing and thinks that he knows. I neither know nor think that I know."* He went on to explain that the admission of ignorance is the first step in attaining truth, knowledge and virtue.

There is nothing that I can present to you as absolute truth. Humans do not get to know absolute truth. Even if I could tell you from direct experience what *God* looks like, you will not *know* until you see and experience *God* for yourself. You would be simply taking my word for it and in that sense subscribing to my supposed authority. No matter what you are told by a teacher or guru, you can't know the truth of the law of rebirth unless you have experienced it consciously and then you have the same problem - finding the words to describe it to someone who has no similar experience with which to draw parallels. This brings up the last point I want to make in this regard. Even if I had learned all of the secrets of the universe, how would I convey them? I would do it like everyone else has, through the use of language.

My father used to say that language is an "honest lie." I don't know where he got it, so I ascribe it to him. No matter how hard you try to explain something you are first conceptualizing, and then creating an image of some idea that only approximates it. Then you are communicating it through the truly inadequate tool of language, which in a sense flattens it out for transmission. It is then to be re-expanded and brought to life through the understanding of the person with whom you are communicating. The words employed will be taken with the meanings assigned to them by the listener, not the speaker. There is an old phrase which takes a somewhat humorous look at this idea and it goes, "I know you believe you understand what you think I said. What I am telling you is that what you heard is not what I meant."

The idea is similar to the concept of compression in computers. We can *zip* a file up by running it through a mathematical algorithm to make it smaller and later unzip it by running through the same formula backwards. If the equation used in the second case is not identical, distortion in the message will result. The equation in this case is the symbolism of the language. The words do not have the exact same meanings to each of us and so to an extent we can expect a distortion of the meaning conveyed.

This loss of dimension and meaning in translation is similar to the phenomena Plato explains in his analogy of the shadows on the cave wall. If you are not familiar with this concept, picture a person in a cave facing to the rear, away from the entrance or any source of light. Activities going on behind him produce shadows on the cave wall. Having no view but that of the shadows, the person will only have the ability to perceive a two dimensional fraction of the happenings creating the phenomena experienced. All depth, definition and color are lost in this translation, leaving only a literal shadow of the three dimensional actuality.

Any thought or idea loses a dimension as it is translated into words. It is then re-constructed in the mind of the listener. It will be different because the consciousness of the listener uses different filters than the speaker, based on their individual life experience. Having familiarity with the size and shapes of the bodies behind him, the observer could conceivably reconstruct some of the activities going on in the cave, in the three dimensional image making faculty of his mind. He is easily led astray however, as anyone who has made shadow animals on the wall for their children can attest.

There is another problem with language, in that it is only useful in sharing common experience. If you are blind from birth and I say to you that the sky is blue, my words fall on equally deaf ears. Without the common experience the words mean nothing. According to James Borg in his work "Body Language"[5] they contain only 7% of the meaning of anything we say. The other parts are tone and emphasis along with cadence and body language. Just think about that for a moment. The words themselves are almost insignificant. The art of sarcasm is the making of a statement while implying the opposite through tone and emphasis with either harmful or comedic intent. The true meaning will be immediately apparent between those who know each other well, and can be completely misunderstood among those outside any particular circle, or even culture.

Emerson said "words impoverish truth." St. Paul said of his revelations that he had heard "unspeakable words." Then he wrote all of his epistles with speak-able words. They were his only tools to relate his impressions and I will be using them as well. The inadequacy of language to convey universal truth is one of the reasons that scripture is written symbolically, as you will see. This idea is so important to keep in mind that it is one of the seven keys with which we will unlock the wisdom of the ages. Knowledge of how this symbolic language will be interpreted by people of various levels of awareness and sensitivity literally shapes the way the stories are told. They are layered with meaning because it is understood by the writers that reading them has to involve interpretation. There is in a sense, *no original meaning* to any scripture that can be ascertained and apprehended by an individual. There are a range of meanings, to be understood by the vast array of people in the world, according to their level of conscious development.

Truth is veiled in symbolism so that without the keys you have a pleasant fable with a simple moral. Once the keys to the symbolism used in the writing are in the possession of the reader as well, then the door is opened to a wealth of knowledge. In the words of Geoffrey Hodson the symbolism is used "to conceal *and reveal* the deeper meaning"[6] (my italics). He also warns us that when we see something incongruous in

---

5   James Borg - *Body Language: 7 Easy Lessons to Master the Silent Language (London: Pearson Education Ltd)*

6   Geoffery Hodson *The Hidden Wisdom of The Holy Bible* (USA: Theosophical Publishing House 1993)

the writing, like someone being rewarded for what would normally be considered bad behavior, it is a hint that a deeper meaning is being presented symbolically.

In order to be able to share these concepts with you we need to define the field of enquiry. As we proceed I will try to make sure that I am clear about the way I am using various terms because you are reading the book I am writing and therefore, we need to use my definitions. Once you understand what I am relating, then you will be able to put it into your own terms and decide whether what I am telling you warrants further investigation.

Above all else, what I will do is provide you with ways to improve your life. When I was in conversation with a friend at work about some of my studies she said, "I couldn't do it!" I asked what she meant, and in answer she said "the perpetual student thing." I protested that I am merely a student of life, and that I was just digging in a little deeper than some. She seemed to accept that more easily.

At another time I was asked directly "Why do you need to know all that stuff?" It took me aback for a moment. From their perspective, it was just study for the sake of study. I found it interesting that the practical application of these principles to everyday life is completely lost on some, and they assume it to be piety for its own sake. Aspiration is certainly a part of it but this is a process which opens with the building of character in the personality. One of the ideas often discussed with regard to spiritual living, is that is it considered by many to be impractical and ill-suited to life in the modern world. Recently, there have been attempts to qualify practical spirituality as the application of some of their system of belief to the world around them, embracing principles which easily apply to daily life. It's a start but this is an incomplete way of living your faith, because you reserve parts of it for a separate *inner life*.

Spiritual Practicality is the integration of your spiritual life, your inner being in its totality, to the practical world. You live spiritually through every experience, because your awareness is changed. The materialistic approach to living in the West is an empty and illusory lifestyle. When you truly live spiritually, you will find that every aspect of your inner life has a practical application in the modern world.

The application of any set of principles to one's life builds character. These teachings carry this idea to its ultimate expression - conscious union with the divine, through a series of recognitions, leading to revelation. Depending on where within the continuum your level of consciousness identifies itself, you will find appropriate meaning in these multi layered teachings to better your understanding and thus, your life. When we learn to move in harmony with life itself, our burden is felt differently.

In all of this, we are exploring *the nature of being and knowing*[7] through teachings that have permeated the mind of man throughout the ages. We will look at evolution but not just biological evolution. We will explore it in all its facets; especially the evolution of consciousness and the evolution of spirit itself.

In the various chapters to come we will be exploring ideas which may seem to be separate topics, with our Seven Keys as common threads that bind all of this knowledge together. These relationships will become clearer as we proceed and so we will, in some cases, find ourselves revisiting certain ideas in greater depth after having first addressed them somewhat superficially in the context of another conversation. This will especially be the case with the subject of the Seven Planes of Manifestation. We will of necessity, explore the various ranges of energetic matter which embrace us on our journey throughout this entire work. It will initially be an ancillary part of many of our topics and then later used to show the interaction of the entire creative process, once we have gained an understanding of the supposedly separate ideas.

We will study the Constitution of Man from the physical entity and its energetic, emotional and mental counterparts, to the Soul or conscious

---

[7]   The definition of metaphysics according to Miriam Webster "a division of philosophy that is concerned with the fundamental nature of reality and being and that includes ontology, cosmology, and often epistemology".

observer at its core. We will also address the spiritual essence at the core of the Soul, which is just another vehicle on a more rarefied plane for the indwelling spiritual essence.

We will study Reincarnation; the process through which that Soul enters the physical world or *incarnates*. It is a cyclical expression that mirrors the creative process in every other aspect of the universe. Through what is known as Esoteric Psychology, or the study of the seven rays, we will examine the influences which color human expression in the physical, mental and astral worlds.

We will look at The Trinity[8] and its expression in man, as well as the various Kingdoms of Nature and their relationships. This will include the emerging Fifth Kingdom - The Kingdom of Souls, Paradise, Nirvana, Mecca, Satori, Heaven, or the Promised Land. These are all expressions of a state of being rather than physical locations. The symbol is in this case mistaken for the idea which it indicates. You will see this evidenced in virtually all of the misunderstandings of the ancient teachings. The words used to symbolize and point the way toward the truth are often mistaken for the truth itself. Joseph Campbell, Author of "A Hero with 1000 Faces" said "The main problem with symbols is that people tend to get lost in the symbol. The problem with myth and the problem with mysticism is that you should not lose the message in the symbol. The message is always of the spirit and when the symbol is taken to be the fact, so that you have to go to Haridwar to get to the source of the Ganges, you have mistaken the message. There is a similar mistake in the notion that you have to go to Israel to reach the Promised Land. This concretization is one of the major deceptions in the western handling of symbols. It is one of the reasons we have lost touch with the perennial message."

---

8   The trinity is the basis for all of the major religions of the world except for Islam, in which the idea is seen as diminishing to the ultimate power of the one God. As we will see, the Ageless Wisdom teaches the trinity as the first expression of this same omnipotent unifying force. The creator is not seen as diminished by the act of creation.

In an introductory work such as this, it will be impossible for me to go into any great depth on this vast array of ideas. Any of them could be the subject of not only an entire book but a lifetime of study. My purpose is to expose you to this entire system of thought in order to better equip you in dealing with your life in general. What I present to you will also make the reading of the occult classics more coherent. Since you are reading this particular book, I know that you have begun a journey that will lead you to all of these ideas eventually. My hope is to ease the confusion that can result from that immersion, by creating a structure or scaffolding that will give shape to these ideas. Your further study will enable you to fill in the blanks more easily if this framework is in place from the beginning. If you have already been introduced to some of these concepts my hope is to show the relationships between them, thus lending clarity that will aid you in understanding and applying them to improve your life and the lives of those around you. To this end I will be pointing you toward sources of more specific and detailed treatments of these subjects as we go.

THE KEYS TO THE MYSTERIES OF "THE AGELESS WISDOM"

Key One – LIFE -There is but One Life.

Key Two – FORM -The One Life expresses itself through matter in order to experience and master form.

Key Three – VIBRATION - All Manifestation is cyclical. It is the result of, and conditioned by, vibration.

Key Four – CONSIOUSNESS - Consciousness is the result of the interaction of spirit and matter and evolves through it.

Key Five – LEVELS - As it is above, so it is below.

Key Six – LIVES - All forms of life embrace lesser forms and are in turn embraced by greater forms.

Key Seven – SYMBOLISM - All Spiritual Teachings are necessarily given in symbolism.

So we have:

One Life
Creating the Manifested universe
Based on Vibration
Resulting in Consciousness
Cycle within Cycle
Life within Life
Represented Symbolically

CHAPTER 1

The Keys

I must admit, I have questioned the form that this information should take and how to present these key ideas within the framework of this book. My first inclination was to weave the information into the chapters and require readers to ferret out for themselves what these keys really are. The other approach would be to just give them to you up front and risk having the simplistic summary given as a precursor being judged too quickly. In other words, you might not read the book if you thought you understood the CliffsNotes. The fact is that these keys are not the teaching, but rather they are a cipher with which the teachings are more readily understood. For this reason I have chosen to bring them out with a simple explanation and then refer back to them as we progress. In a sense the book will explain the keys, as the keys explain the book.

It is this approach that I believe will suit our purpose most efficiently. Like any cipher, having these keys facilitates the understanding of an encoded message. Without one another, they are almost equally useless - unless of course one is able to discern the meaning on one's own, in essence cracking the code for herself. This is really the job of every individual investigator on the path. Of course, a few hints along the way as to the deeper meaning of a multi-layered message can save an enormous amount of time. There is nothing wrong with solving a tedious mathematical problem with a simple formula, provided you understand what the formula does. That is the essence of what these more or less universal truths unlock in the wisdom stories that have been passed down through the ages. I intentionally qualified the idea of universal truth because the human consciousness can only comprehend relative truth. Within the consciousness of a human being, these threads of wisdom take on a very universal appearance. They can lead us to a state unlike normal waking consciousness and a little closer to the true awareness of unity. Kept in mind while reading scriptures, legends and myths, we see them as the hidden threads tying all of these tales together. There comes to the reader a moment of recognition. The symbolic and holistic nature of the scriptures of the world comes into focus and with that comes the revelation that they are all teaching us the same things. They simply grew out of, and were affected by, differing cultures and so carry the colorings and emotional sentiments of those cultures. The underlying message is the same. My hope is that through the reading of this simple work you will have opened before you the Path to Enlightenment in a way that makes it real and possible for you.

These "Keys" are basic, yet somewhat abstract ideas that you will see repeated as we explore the body of the Ageless Wisdom, which lies at the core of all of the major systems of religious philosophy. They are reflections of truths that have lost dimension, but still allude to their source. You will see them expressed over and over throughout the rest of our exploration, leading you to an understanding of the meaning and depth contained within these seemingly simple ideas. If they are in fact universal truths, at least as far as the human consciousness is capable of understanding truth, then we will see them expressed on all levels of manifestation. This is an expression of what is known as *The Law of Correspondences*, and with these keys we will be able to build a foundation upon which all of the rest of what I share with you will stand. Viewed through the lens of this simple hierarchy of ideas, the wisdom in the teachings that have pervaded every human culture comes into clear relief against the backdrop of noise that is created by their very misunderstanding. Initially I will be referencing them often and later leave the recognition to the reader so as not to be too repetitive.

Key One – LIFE - There is but One Life.

All of the keys to the understanding of this universal wisdom can be boiled back down to this one simple statement. It is the unifying principle in all of creation. All is alive, and all of the varied forms of manifestation are drawn from this one infinite pool of life to create the universe we see - and all that escapes our grasp as well. It is you and me, and the space between us, teeming with life and energy. Science tells us that there is enough energy within a cubic centimeter of empty space to boil away the oceans of the earth if we could truly harness it.[9] Empty space is far from empty. Our perception is far from complete.

Key Two – FORM - The One Life expresses itself through matter, in order to experience and master form.

There are only two discernible reasons for this infinite sea of divine awareness to create on any material plane (and they are all material). They are (1) to experience the world of form, and (2) to express its awareness in that world. This is the Evolutionary Impulse[10] and is an expression of what is called *The Law of Necessity*. Deity must create.

Key Three – VIBRATION - All manifestation is cyclical; it is the result of, and conditioned by, vibration.

The world around you is vibrating from every corner of existence. These vibrations sometimes harmonize, and sometimes they do not, but patterns emerge out of chaos like the autogenic effects we see in fluid dynamics.[11] This is impersonal and factual, as it is in all of the

---

[9] This *Zero Point Energy* (or ZPE) represents what is known as the ground state of any quantum system. It is related to the uncertainty principle and results in motion even at absolute zero - the coldest possible temperature.

[10] Andrew Cohen – *Evolutionary Enlightenment: A New Path to Spiritual Awakening* (New York: Select Books, 2011)

[11] Terrence W. Deacon - *Incomplete Nature : How Mind Emerged From Matter* (New York: W.W. Norton & Company. 2011)

keys. Science defines heat, and therefore energy itself, by molecular movement. There is perpetual motion in the universe at scales that we cannot imagine. The microwave background radiation famously and accidentally discovered by Arno Penzias and Robert Woodrow Wilson are reverberations of the big bang. This is science's version of Genesis, and since that moment when time, space and matter began, it has all been vibrating.

Key Four – CONSCIOUSNESS - Consciousness is the result of the interaction of spirit and matter, and evolves through it.

The majority of the religious traditions of the world are based on the same trinity of creation. We will go into this idea in great depth later, but in all cases there is a male principle related to will and seen as spirit, and a female principle related to matter, and encompassing activity and expression. The third is the result of that interaction, which is the principle of consciousness, represented in Christianity as the "Son." Spirit pervades matter with a fragment of itself resulting in consciousness. Not life, for all is alive, but in sentience or awareness. Consciousness requires form. It evolves through the progressive mastery of its medium of expression.

Key Five – LEVELS - As it is above, so it is below.

Vibrations manifest in repeating patterns and harmonics. Through these patterns of vibration we see the emergence of mathematical relationships. The doubling of an audio frequency results in the first harmonic or, in the most common form of musical notation, the octave note. There are relationships between the various planes of existence we will study. Just as every note necessarily has its counterpart in every octave, there are things that we will see repeatedly expressed on varied levels of physical manifestation - and consciousness as well. Cycles repeat within cycles; worlds within worlds.

Key Six – LIVES - All forms of life embrace lesser forms and are in turn embraced by greater forms.

Now we see that in addition to worlds within worlds, we have lives within lives, embraced by the One Life. In this context the idea of a "greater" form of life simply means a more complex and encompassing one that, as we will see, is the result of a higher level of consciousness. The earth is a living organism; it is an assemblage and community of the differing life forms that make up its totality. It is the macrocosm (big universe) to our microcosm (little universe). It embraces us on our journey as we embrace the billions of varied cellular level lives, as well as the hitch hikers and stowaways we take along for the ride within our own smaller system. There are many organisms within your body that are decidedly not human, such as the over one hundred trillion microbes of over four hundred different types in your digestive tract alone.[12] From the perspective of those lives, you are the macrocosm. These are separate little creatures living within you who are as crucial to your survival as you are to theirs. I hope you are beginning to see how these ideas are all couched within one another.

Key Seven – SYMBOLISM - Spiritual teachings are necessarily given in symbolism.

Spiritual realities can only be experienced firsthand. For this reason we cannot do anything but to use symbols to point at these abstract truths from a number of differing perspectives. The level of comprehension is dependent on the level of conscious awareness of the perceiver. I cannot overstress this idea, and it can be the most helpful way of looking at spiritual and philosophical teachings.

---

[12]   Bill Bryson - *A Short History of Nearly Everything* (USA: Broadway Books 2003)

With these concepts in mind, we will now take a look at the way spiritual truth has been communicated over the course of ages, and what it is that these teachings are trying to show us.

Remember that when we talk and think in symbols we are placing something between ourselves and reality – something protective, interpretive and significant, but something nevertheless veiling and hiding.

The Master Djwahl Kuhl

CHAPTER 2

Hidden Meaning

Where we begin really has more to do with our seventh key than with the first, or even with the first few. The fact is that we need to establish the reasoning behind how I will present this information. I have the same issues to contend with that have been the obstacle to spiritual truth for every teacher. That is, describing the indescribable through loose allegory and parable - or in a word, *symbolism*.

With the birth of scientific materialism and the overwhelming acceptance the scientific community enjoys, except where it is politically expedient to ignore it, the universe has been reduced to a random mechanism governed by impersonal laws. They did get half of that right, incidentally. The laws are completely impersonal. In this system of thought, matter is seen as the font of all being. If something cannot be proven to exist materially, it is not *real*. This artificially firm stance is far from being seated in unimpeachable evidence and theoretical physics posits some very contrary and even counter intuitive ideas. There are things going on within our world that defy our senses. We have to be able to conceptualize these ideas in a space that is abstracted from what we see as the material world.

We are going to explore the Esoteric Principles which reside within, and form the core of some very spiritual concepts, as well as their corollaries in the quantum world. That leads to the first real question. What is Esotericism? This is going to be a tough one right out of the gate. This word is relatively meaningless to most people but maybe we can actually turn that to our advantage. We can define it for them, and perhaps refine the meaning for those who have been familiarized with the term. When you define something, you define what it is, as well as what it is not. Something that is light is known not to be dark. Something that is green is obviously not red or blue. In the case of something for which the meaning is illusive, the more we can put into the column of what it is not, the better we make the definition. When the opposite of something is fairly clear, it can be easier to define that and then work backwards.

In the case of the word esoteric it might be useful to define it in contradistinction to its opposite "exoteric." Even though there may be fewer people who have heard that word, it is easier to define and understand. The prefix "exo" means outer (as in exterior) and "eso" means inner. The exoteric nature is the outer appearance of something and the esoteric is its inner essence. That's the surface of it but let's go a bit deeper. It is going to be the subject of extensive analysis throughout this work but we need to get a handle on it up front so we are all on the same page as we go.

Exoteric is: measurable by the senses, or by some extension of the senses, like a microscope. It has form, height, depth and width. It is manifested, tangible and a part of the physical world that science has always acknowledged. This is covered by the physical sciences or *physics* as pioneered by Sir Isaac Newton and Francis Bacon.

Esoteric is: hidden, beneath - not plain to the senses or measurable. Albert Einstein tells us in his laws of the conservation of matter and energy that all is truly of one essence and this essence moves in and out of physical expression. If matter is formed from energy then energy is the underlying cause of the physical or material world. If we release the energy as we do when we burn something, we can easily see that matter is the source of the energy being released and we see that much of the material is lost with the release of the energy. Matter cannot be both the cause and result of the physical world, so we have to look at the energies that are its precursor. We will be exploring those energies and so, the world of causes or what is known as *metaphysics*. This term was coined by the students of Aristotle when they were arranging his writings and placed his papers on the underlying causes of the universe after his papers on Physical Science. Meta (beyond or after) and phusika (physical). He himself never used the word. He referred to these teachings as "First Philosophy."

We are actually talking about the world of quantum physics; which to this day is still considered theoretical physics, although direct experimentation has proven much of the early theory. The quantum field is an interesting term and for science a really strange pursuit, if you think about the rules of the hypothesis. The interesting part is that they *see* the evidence of something like an electron in the mathematics. This is in some cases, decades before they are actually able to detect it with their equipment. They foray into the intangible. This is where science and spirituality begin to merge and science becomes very uncomfortable. The current pursuit is for evidence of the existence of dark matter, which is supposed to be more than five times as abundant within the universe as what we call matter. With the inclusion of dark energy, it represents up to 95% of the substance of the universe, and is one possible explanation for its accelerating expansion. The scientific community has reduced the physical world to the relationships of four forces and a handful of particles.[13]

The last of these to be theorized is that elusive particle of matter, the Higgs Boson. Again, based upon relationships leaving holes in what is called mathematical symmetry, they *know* it is there and have been looking for empirical evidence of it. On March 13th 2013 research at the CERN large hadron collider revealed the existence of this long sought after Higgs Boson that is thought to give mass to all matter in the Universe. It has been nicknamed the "God Particle" because it is thus

---

[13]   (Strong nuclear force weak nuclear force, gravitation and electromagnetism are the forces. The particles are various quarks leptons and bosons).

responsible for all material manifestation. All matter has mass, which is actually a measure of its gravitational influence.[14]

So in a sense we have two dimensions, one within the other, coexisting. There are actually many but for the moment we can stick with this over simplification until we have some other concepts developed. We know about the physical or exoteric world. The esoteric world we will have to deal with like we do with quantum physics; theoretically. Christ said "The Kingdom of God is within you." (Luke 17:21) This is the esoteric world. It will not be discovered outside of ourselves. The Oracle of Delphi advised man "Know thyself and thou hast read the world."

Reality or Actuality?

There are as many realities as there are units of consciousness. Each person has his or her own reality. There is only one actuality. Reality is how we perceive the world, actuality is what truly is. So reality can be seen as exoteric and actuality as esoteric.

Remember, when I write I will be necessarily using words that have certain meanings to me and when you read you will be filtering what is said through your own meanings. There is a truth involved but I (as a human consciousness) have colored that through my own experience and interpreted it. Next, I work within the limitations of the words I have at my disposal to convey that now imperfect truth to you. Then you reinterpret it for yourself and if you try to pass it on there will be another layer or layers added, veiling further the truth of the matter. If this is true even when I say something we are all familiar with, like "blue" and more so with a qualifier like "sky blue," just imagine for a moment the complications that arise when we get to a term like "God" or even "Life" but those are the topics we will be discussing.

---

[14] Science to this day struggles to explain Gravity. It is defined as the force of attraction between objects with mass. We know how to predict its effects but not their origin.

Actuality is the pure condition, reality is the way we *realize* it. Actuality *is* and reality *is created* by each individual consciousness. The suffix *ize* represents an action as in the word *categorize*. When we realize something we make it real; but only for our own consciousness. When I realize something, it is an internal change that has no effect on others unless I relate it to them and they *realize* it for themselves. We all see things differently because to an extent, we are the product of our experiences, conditioning and thought processes. We see things differently as adults than we did as children. We interpret a movie's meaning differently from the person who sat next to us in the theatre. If you go back and re-read a book you read years ago you will interpret it differently because you have changed. The book is the same. Nothing is of intrinsic value. One man's meat is another man's poison but in actuality it is neither meat, nor poison.

Esotericism has been defined as a synthesis of religion, philosophy, and science; the same three disciplines that define pure Theosophy. Our goal here is to explore all three, but we will not be approaching them in the way you might expect. Within science we will be approaching psychology from its original meaning, the knowledge of the Soul, not the science of behavioral modification that it has become. In religion we will be looking at the mystical teachings which are at their source. Anyone who does not believe that there is an esoteric teaching that is given to the true devotees and not to the rank and file of the faith is deluding themselves. Jesus taught his inner circle directly and the masses were given the teachings in symbols and parables. He stated this explicitly to his disciples[15] and that is in direct support of our seventh key. We will be looking closely at the symbolism employed because all scriptures are subject to the interpretation of the reader and they are pointing the way to something intangible, as we discussed before. With regard to philosophy we will be taking the posture of the word itself "lover of truth." We are seeking the core truths that are depicted in all of the world religions, spiritual disciplines and philosophies.

---

[15] "To you it has been granted to know the mysteries of the Kingdom of Heaven, but to them it has not been granted… This is why I speak to them in parables: Though seeing, they do not see; though hearing, they do not hear or understand." (Matthew 13:11).

"The most beautiful and profound emotion we can experience is the sensation of the mystical. It is the sower of all true science. He to whom this emotion is a stranger, who can no longer wonder and stand wrapped in awe, is as good as dead. To know that what is impenetrable to us really exists, manifesting itself as the highest wisdom and the most radiant beauty which our dull faculties can comprehend only in their most primitive forms; this knowledge, this feeling is at the center of true religiousness."

Albert Einstein.

CHAPTER 3

The Ageless Wisdom

The wisdom that this work is based upon has no known or verifiable origin. It is said to predate the existence of humanity on this planet. Now, that can be taken as a threat to the credibility of what I am here to share with you. It potentially opens the door to fantastical stories of any kind I may have a whim to spin. I can assure you that this will not prove to be the case and you will see the teachings in your surroundings. You do not have to believe what I say because what I am claiming to be pointing to are universal truths. If they are what they are purported to be then you should see evidence of them everywhere. This Ageless Wisdom is the embodiment of all that we will discuss and is known as the source and the wisdom of all of the world's religions. Its symbolism is the thread that runs through all of the teachings passed down through the ages. This is the hidden world of meaning and it is open to any who care to explore or expose those truths to her own conscious enquiry; to become the Esotericist. If you keep in mind The Seven Keys, you will unlock a greater understanding from these ancient teachings.

For the Esotericist, this is the search for truth, wherever that search may lead. She is an open minded investigator not a seeker, for a seeker tends to find what she is looking for. She is a scientist and detective looking unbiased into the mysteries of the universe and creating a mental and emotional construct of what she finds, in an attempt to convey those unspeakable secrets to others.

This is what scientists have been doing since the dawn of their art and they are coming back around to some of the same conclusions the sages have asserted for millennia. There is a tendency to say they took the long way around but the empirical sciences are in their infancy - having only been explored for a few hundred years. The leaps in the last one hundred or so are incredible. The data gathered through the mathematical research in particle physics has forced these empiricists to explore, with their imaginations, a world much different from that which we experience with our senses. They are truly Esotericists in that they are searching the world of causes and meaning. In the course of that search they have theorized the existence of intangible vibrating energy packets called quanta. We have been taught for ages that all is energy and now science is beginning to accept this deeply esoteric truth through its own controlled investigative methods.

This is the most comprehensive study that a person can undertake. Fortunately, you do not have to be a physicist or a theologian to pursue it. Madam Helena Petrovna Blavatsky (hereafter referred to as Madame Blavatsky or simply HPB) said "there is no religion greater than truth." We are told that this teaching is the font of the world's religions and in my experience I have found that it rejects none of the tenets of these various faiths. Whether it is their source, or a system derived and distilled from them is of no real consequence. Truth is truth whether or not its source can be ascertained or reasoned through. It does not care whether it is "apprehended" or understood and interestingly is not encumbered by its apprehension. Madame Blavatsky referred to this doctrine of truth as *The Secret Doctrine* and said of its wisdom,

> *"The teachings belong neither to the Hindu, the Zoroastrian,*
> *the Chaldean nor the Egyptian religion. Neither to Buddhism*

> *Islam Judaism nor Christianity exclusively; The Secret Doctrine is the essence of all these. Sprung from it in their origins, the various religious schemes are now made to merge back into their original element, out of which every mystery and dogma has grown, developed and become materialized."*

I see in the religious teachings of the world, culturally colored expressions of the same universal truths. *These truths existed prior to their recording and acceptance as some one or other spiritual doctrine.* One plus one equaled two before man came up with the symbols used to state it. What any particular writer may have tuned into in order to contact this truth is going to occupy much of our time; their identity, very little. The end result of this contact with the truth is the creation of a religious doctrine, as interpreted by an individual or a small group and then disseminated through an entire culture or a group within that culture. This new doctrine is remembered, reinforced and empowered by the use of ritual and allegory. These *separate* systems originate in the same source, but have come through different channels and cultures and so, appeal to the wide variety of human personalities we have across the face of the earth.

At their core they all have the truth. It is their source and it has been intuited by some human or super human mind. In each case they have veiled it and colored it through their cultural programming and thus distorted it, so none has the pure and whole truth. Because it is their source, none is bereft of truth either.

The guides of the race have been described as Gods walking among men in all of the ancient texts. The work of Erich Von Daniken and others assumes these must have been alien visitors arriving on rocket ships, but The Ageless Wisdom tells us that these beings had no need of spaceships to transport their bodies here. They were moving as consciousness, which can project itself at will and manifest a physical body from the materials available. No matter what religious doctrine may resonate within you it is hard to characterize God as an earthling, and so "He" has an extraterrestrial origin.

The Brotherhood

Traveling at the speed of thought, and arriving on this planet to guide infant humanity approximately 18 million years ago during what is known as the Lemurian Epoch, was a brotherhood of highly evolved beings who then formed the Spiritual Hierarchy of this planet. According to the Secret Doctrine, the Lemurian race inhabiting the earth at that time was the third root race created in our system.[16] Lemurians were enormous, and only possessed a germ of mind. They were basically animal man. This group of spiritual guides arrived to hasten the process of the evolution of the consciousness within them. These are the extra-terrestrials who helped man create things like the pyramids and other ancient wonders. The first two root races of humanity had no dense physical form and the Stanzas of Dyzan[17] refer to "watermen." Now evolution had provided the appropriate form and infant humanity was born. These were the first "suitable" bodies to serve as vehicles for the human consciousness to inhabit, and use, for the furtherance of conscious evolution.

Now, we are supposed to be dealing with universal truths and according to our Fifth Key, we should be able to see parallels above and below as we go. As we will see, the development of the individual reflects the development of the race. Early humanity had their focus on their physical bodies and we can see a parallel in the life and development of a child. Their experiences are centered in the physical experience of the body and they have no concept of a separate mind or emotional nature. There is further information about this era available for those who have an interest, but my purpose in bringing it up at this point is to show the patterns of evolution on varying scales. A physically oriented person even today is said to have Lemurian aspects of his consciousness dominant.

---

[16] For a full explanation of the root races and sub races see The Secret Doctrine Volume 2 Anthropogenisis. Helena Blavatsky - *The Secret Doctrine: Synthesis of Science, Religion and Philosophy Vol. II.* (London: The Theosophical Publishing Company, 1888)

[17] Helena Blavatsky - *The Secret Doctrine: Synthesis of Science, Religion and Philosophy Vol. I* (London: Theosophical Publishing Company1888

As humanity developed in capacity, the emotional nature began to take on an increasing role and we see this evidenced in the stories of the Atlantian era or epoch. This encompassed an enormous period of time and emotional expression was turned toward the selfish use of power on every level. The deeper levels of individuation lend a greater sense of self and unguided, this can produce horrors. The teen years can be associated with this Atlantian consciousness and we all realize the difficulty in dealing with the emotional rollercoaster ride this can be. Nothing matters at that stage except for the individual's *wants*. The sense of self is overwhelming and becomes selfishness. At its peak Atlantis made strides in agriculture and animal domestication - working together for the common good. During the decadence and decline of this era, the guides of the race who had walked openly among humanity had to drop back out of sight. The open teaching of these doctrines without first qualifying the student led to abuses of the abilities thus attained for selfish ends. The ruling castes had begun to restrict the impartation of these powerful teachings based on family and political interests, rather than the qualifications and evolutionary status of the individual. The Atlantian consciousness is an emotionally charged one and emotions cloud the clear light of reason. Again, if we look at an individual child or teen, they have a stage of selfish wants and a complete disregard for the others who may be affected by their actions. We need guidance to show us the way but there comes a time when the choice has to be made by each individual. Free will in this context does exist and we can know *right* and choose *wrong* anyway.

Humanity had to work things out for ourselves and it was going to take time. With these necessities, the training of disciples went underground into the Mystery Schools. From Atlantis, which is said to have been overcome by the sea, they went to India and Egypt. Water or weather are symbols of the emotional nature and the emotional Atlantian race could be seen as having been destroyed by their misuse of astral energies, or incompetence in the mastery of the Astral Plane.

The Mystery Schools

In Egypt the teachings resurfaced under the rule of the fourth Amenhotep. He was known as the Mystic King and ruled Egypt around 1300BC. He was considered by many the first idealist, realist, and monotheist. He symbolized his God with a golden disk and called him Aton (sometimes spelled Aten). This is an obvious reference to the sun and he used to salute the rising sun with his arms outstretched, producing a shadow that looked like a cross with a loop at the top. This is the modern ankh, called at the time the Crux Ansata. (also the handled cross or the cross of life). Interestingly, he saw even the sun itself as a symbol and worshiped the *energy within the disk*.[18]

He ruled with his wife Nefertiti and took the name Akhenaton or "Servant of Aton," the one true God. He was the father of Tutakhenaton, who took the name Tutankhamen when he became Pharaoh after Akhenaton's death. This was an indication of the turning of Egypt back from the worship of Aton to Amen Rah by the priestly caste, with what was likely undue influence over the boy king. Other actions were taken after his death to destroy remnants of the monotheistic doctrines adopted under Akhenaton, including the destruction of Amkara, the "City of Aton" from which he ruled Egypt, after realizing that Thebes would never fully accept this new inclusive doctrine.

During his reign of only 18 years he presided over the mystery schools of Egypt which taught: healing, levitation, and psychic power, but as byproducts of development, not as goals. They were taught purification of character and the spiritual constitution of man, the human being as a Soul - all of the things I am going to share with you in these pages, and much more.

Quote from Cambridge History Volume II

---

[18]   This is known in the Ageless Wisdom as the Central Spiritual Sun and referred in the ancient prayer known as the Gayatri

> *The modern world has yet to value this man who, in an era so remote and under conditions so remote became the world's first individual monotheist, and first prophet of internationalism. The most remarkable figure in the ancient world.*

He saw Aton as *The One God*, expressing through all of the faiths, not exclusive of them. When he died and the religious establishment came back to power, the mystery schools again went underground. Students had to be picked tested and schooled, then they often returned to their communities to teach. To this day, this is the method by which spiritual students are trained. These mystery schools have survived the political and social changes of all of the cultures of man because the guides of the race are ever cognizant of the state of humanity as a whole and adjust the presentation of spiritual knowledge to the level of its capacity to understand. Natalie Banks, in her book *The Golden Thread*[19] tells us,

> "*The ancient mystery temples, first established in Atlantis and continued in Egypt, and later in Greece and Rome, became the main repositories of esoteric teaching. Other centers of the mystery rites were those of Chaldea and Persia, from which arose the Mythraic Cult, the Druidic mysteries celebrated in Britain and Gaul, and the Odinic rites of the Scandinavian and Germanic Countries. There were also state mysteries among the Inca, Maya, and Aztec Ancient civilizations.*" As Manly Hall remarks, "*No nation or age has been without its mystery schools.*"

In Greece they established the Theraputi. In Palestine they were the Essenes, who were responsible for the Dead Sea Scrolls. The Judaic religion was founded on these principles because Moses was trained as an Egyptian. They were schooled in principles which seemed to be "magic" to the common man. Think of the story in Exodus in which Aaron's staff turned into a serpent that devoured the serpents of the Egyptian Magicians. The symbol of the serpent universally represents consciousness, as illustrated in Eden where it was the impetus towards

---

[19]   Natalie Banks - *The Golden Thread* (New York: Lucis Publishing Company 1963)

the gaining of the knowledge of good and evil. The Magi at the birth of Christ were just that, magicians; highly conscious beings aware on levels far beyond that of their contemporaries.

They were the Gnostics (true knowledge) of their age and were said to have a deeper understanding of Spirituality than the average religious devotee. The Rosicrucian order finds its history and origin in the mystery schools of Egypt and The Masonic Order as well. All of their rites and ceremonies have an esoteric meaning, although much of this may be lost on the average Mason. This wisdom is too far reaching for it to be carried in a single doctrine and that would be inappropriate because we are all influenced by the same energies, but in different ways. These tendencies will make one school of thought more resonant with an individual than another. They are all built on an aspect of the truth with which some spiritual leader found resonance, resulting in its exoteric expression in the religious dogma as it was presented to, and accepted by, the masses.

There are seven major schools of Yoga, each with a different approach to union. Each geared toward a different type of person and or a different period in human History. They are:

Hatha Yoga – This approach involves physical discipline such as Martial Arts or what people normally think of as "Yoga." It seeks union through the perfection and control of the physical body.

Bhakti Yoga – This is a devotional and often religious expression. Christianity and Hinduism are forms of Bhakti Yoga.

Karma Yoga – The Yoga of action or service.

Laya Yoga – The study of Kundalini and its application.

Tantra Yoga – An eclectic approach often associated with sexual expression.

Raja Yoga – (the Yoga of Kings) Mental discipline and meditation.

Jnana Yoga – Wisdom and intuitional; uniting the mind and heart approach. Wisdom is knowledge lovingly applied.

There has also been the relatively recent emergence of another form of yoga. **Agni Yoga** – Purification by fire, also known as the yoga of synthesis.

There are seven great modifications of energy known as the Seven Rays and they express themselves through all of creation. Each person is affected and influenced by these rays in differing combinations, which we will address later on in Chapters 11 and 12. What it means to us right now is that no one approach will work for every human being. It is the reason for the differing cultural approaches to Deity which we see expressed through the world's religious disciplines. Each of these will spark differing levels of interest in every person and one of them will constitute the *path of least resistance* for each of us. They are all based upon an idea of union with the divine through the application of some sort of discipline of self-discovery, or more accurately, self-mastery. They all express this union as a combination of all of the paths with particular emphasis on one of them.

The universe is like a hologram containing all of the aspects of the whole in every part. This is what is meant by the phrase "man is made in God's image." If man truly knows himself (the microcosm) he will know God (the macrocosm). This philosophy was brought before humanity in the teachings of Hermes Trismegistus (the thrice greatest) and can be phrased in the few simple words of our Fifth Key. "As it is above, so it is below." HPB told us that we will know truth through the Law of Correspondences. Analogy will be a tool that we incorporate throughout this work. What I can see in man I can posit of God. Anything that I can see evidenced upon levels I am capable of perceiving, I can extrapolate on levels I cannot perceive, with at least relative comfort.

Our Sixth Key gives us the occult truth that will hold our attention much of the time and it is that "All forms of life embrace lesser forms and are in turn embraced by greater forms."

We are all holons or whole/parts. The word was coined by Arthur Koestler in his book "The Ghost in the Machine"[20] and incorporated by Ken Wilber in his work as well. Each one of us is a whole human being and simultaneously a functional part of the human race. Each cell in my body is a living being, and if its needs are met it can live independently, outside of my body. We donate our blood to another person and these individual living cells become a functional part of that other *organism*.

The New Presentation

The Ageless Wisdom has taken many shapes and forms in the mystery schools and in the religions of the world. It is usually interpreted by some great light, and colored by the culture and society in which he lives, but you don't need him, or me, or anyone else. This truth can be intuited directly through meditation. HPB said the student learns by "self-devised and self-induced methods." It is The Tao, the way, or the path, and it is up to each of us to find it. The level of consciousness of every human being is unique, and yet we do have groupings of people with similar capacities and tendencies, so the teaching comes in evolving presentations over time.

In 1825 the spiritual guides of the race came together, as they do every 100 years and decided on a three stage presentation. This was based in part on the pending changing of the age of Pisces to Aquarius. Just as the months progress through the cycle of the twelve zodiacal constellations or signs, there is another much longer progression in the reverse order through these same symbols. This is based on the imperfect rotation of the earth in the plane of its orbit around the sun. There is also a very slow wobble in the spin which, in combination with its orbit, effectively changes the moment of each equinox and solstice by about 20 minutes every year. This is called the precession of the equinoxes by astronomers and it is given significance by astrologers over the consciousness of the race as a whole. The energies from these great beings symbolized by

---

[20]   Arthur Koestler – *The Ghost in the Machine* (USA: Random House 1982)

the Zodiacal signs (remember, all is alive) affect the race in a similar fashion to the way we view these influences for the individual in the smaller cycle of a year.

This "New Age" started in 1898. Each period or age is approximately 2160 years long and each is said to have a different effect on man's consciousness. If considered in the same way that the monthly cycles occur, the *cusp* or transition period in which both energies are powerfully present, is hundreds of years long. When we look around ourselves in this transition, we see the turmoil of these conflicting influences as they are mixed and blended. We are experiencing the birth pangs of a new age. There are the reactionary forces that fight change and cling to what we will see as Piscean dogma on one side, and the liberal nuts that want to shove change down our throats and drag us, kicking and screaming, into a new level of conscious awareness on the other. Neither approach is practical because change is inevitable but relies on a change in awareness, so it cannot be forced. We must also keep what works from the old ways while we innovate and implement new ones.

Let's take a look at the passing of the last few of these ages starting with Taurus. To go back further becomes less practical in our context because of the lack of reliable written history. We are trying to tie the influences to behavior in order to illustrate their connection to the human consciousness. In order to do this we must let our imaginations travel back some 6000 years. The Hindu tradition was well under way and the savior of that period was seen in the personage of Krishna. In each of these ages a two word phrase is said to symbolize the view of deity from the perspective of the human consciousness. In Taurus the phrase was "I have." Idolatry ruled the era, and God or divinity was seen in things or totems. Statues were seen not as representations of divinity, but as divine themselves. The cow or ox, representing Taurus, was revered. Abraham's parents were Idol makers and his teaching of the one God, (interestingly, in about the same period as Akhenaton) offers humanity the vehicle of transition to the next *age.*

We move over the course of two millennia into the age of Aries, and what will become the Hebrew doctrine is born and thrives. Moses, who saw God as a presence or "an all-consuming fire" reports to his followers that the "I am" sent him. This is the phrase that characterizes this new age and this new level of awareness. In the shadow of Mount Sinai he saw the Israelites retrogress to the worship of the Golden Calf.[21] Gold, a symbol of the materialistic view of the age of Taurus, further represented by the appropriate form of the calf, demonstrated an unwillingness to progress into this new age. Sheep and sheppard's now become the symbols used in scripture and we see the use of lamb's blood to anoint and identify the homes of the believers in the new age so the curse of death would "pass over" them. God is not experienced as *in things* but is now seen as a Divine presence or consciousness permeating all of creation. This is pure *being* and the human expression of that divine idea is "I am."

Two thousand years of this influence and it yields to a new phase ushered in by the so called lamb of God. We enter Pisces and he tells his followers that he will make them "fishers of men." The new Phrase: "I believe." Blind belief takes hold and people don't wonder why, they just follow tradition; God fearing and blinded, because of the concurrent dominance of the Sixth Ray of devotion. Under these overriding influences the church runs the earth. Man does not know God, he just believes. The good side of this stage is that we awaken to the Christ consciousness and compassion that dwell deep within the human heart. Pisces is a water sign and as we will see later on water and weather are always associated with emotions. Interestingly during this age man conquers the seas and a huge barrier to his reach and his consciousness is overcome. The entire world concept was changed forever by this mastery.

In 1898 we entered into the Age of Aquarius, "The bearer of the waters of knowledge." This is an air sign, and five years later in 1903 the Wright brothers take their first flight and we start the conquest of air and space. The Phrase "I know" is to characterize this new era of human consciousness and we begin the slow process of moving from blind belief

---

21   The Old Testament - Exodus Chapter 32

to knowledge. It is at this stage that the Theosophical Society is formed and we see analysis of spiritual principles, and a responsible inquiry into ideas that seem to defy conventional logic. Mental systems like Science of Mind and self-development movements spring up and flourish. We will *know* God in this new age and the path to this realization is an interior one, for it is our essence.

The spiritual guides of the race have revealed the teachings in a progression that has been appropriate to the capacity of human consciousness, at these varying stages, to receive the truth. At the turn of the 20th century there was a flood of information coming to humanity by way of teachers like Madame Blavatsky, Rudolph Steiner, and Annie Besant, who were in the direct tutelage of Spiritual Masters like Morya, Koot Humi, and Djwahl Kuhl. Of this new approach to spiritual pursuits, Madame Blavatsky remarked "A Theosophist belongs to no sect, no cult, no religion, and no creed, and yet belongs to each and all."

In 1919 Alice A. Bailey began a thirty year collaboration with The Master Djwahl Kuhl which produced a series of twenty-four books. This is, in my judgment, the most important contribution to the exploration of consciousness and the Ageless Wisdom at the core of the mysteries of the universe that came out of this period of enlightenment.

It makes me wonder sometimes when I realize what was going on in the world of science in this same period; what has happened to us? Where is that spark of brilliance? Where is that spiritual aspiration now? We have been distracted by shiny objects, and now we are entering an age where information is at our literal fingertips. We have access to almost everything almost all of the time but we are taking selfies. Aquarius is in full swing but many of us seem to be sleeping through it and it's time to wake up now. As I am writing this draft we are in the seventh week of the "Occupy Wall St." demonstrations. In this short period of time this movement (that is really only asking for fairness) has spread over the entire country and there are solidarity protests around the world. This truly organic shift in consciousness may be the most positive indication of this pending awakening we have seen to date.

So, how do we know all of this is true? How can you believe anything I tell you in the rest of these pages? The fact is that none of this can be verified. We don't know. This is purported to be 18 million year old knowledge. There are those who would testify to it but the only way to know is to look at the fruit of the tree. Consciousness evolves, as reflected in our Fourth Key. These things are evident in our world and we will see throughout this work that much of it is much more prevalent than you might have thought.

My advice is to be wary and observant. Think for yourself and don't follow anyone who demands blind obedience. Be an open minded investigator, rather than a seeker. Treat this as a hypothesis and you will not get stuck in any one aspect of it. I hope to keep the attitude of Djwahl Kuhl as I write and leave the responsibility for discerning the truth with you.

He said;

> *The books that I have written are sent out with no claim for their acceptance. They may or may not be correct true and useful. It is for you to ascertain their truth by right practice and by the exercise of the intuition.*

"I do not believe that matter is inert, acted upon by an outside force. To me it seems that every atom is possessed by a certain amount of primitive intelligence. Look at the thousands of ways in which atoms of hydrogen combine with those of other elements, forming the most diverse substances. Do you mean to say they do this without intelligence? Atoms in harmonious and useful relation assume beautiful or interesting shapes and colours, or give forth a pleasant perfume, as if expressing their satisfaction gathered together in certain forms. The atoms constitute animals of the lower order. Finally they combine in man, who represents the total intelligence of all the atoms."

Thomas Edison

CHAPTER 4

The Evolution Of Consciousness

Now that we have set the stage, I would like to start the body of our discussion with an examination of consciousness. I am not going to restrict it to human consciousness, although we are going to spend quite a bit of time on that later. In its broadest sense consciousness can be defined as *response to contact*. We want to be open to as universal a definition of all of these ideas as we can muster because it will help us tie them together as we go.

Evolution has somehow become a controversial subject. When I was a kid that was considered the best idea for how life has come to appear in all of its varied forms over billions of years. We also knew that at church (I was raised Catholic) they said God made everything. It didn't seem like they were pushing the idea that God made everything exactly the way it is now and did it only 6000 years ago. This idea is based in part on calculations made by Reverend James Usher.[22] I never knew who Reverend Usher was and I guess the idea that someone would try to decide the date of the creation of everything by counting back the generations listed by one culture alone would have seemed silly even to a kid. The fight is obviously over whether Man was evolved from the primates or was created as himself, perfect and whole. As you will begin to see with many of these divisive arguments, I believe the ideas are not mutually exclusive. It all depends on what you see as the evolving entity. Who is the "I" who is evolving? And, how are we looking at that evolution?

I see evolution as the perfect form of creation. It is the most intelligent design possible. Once started, the system creates, and has created, countless forms through which the indwelling life may express itself. The One Life that is the unifying factor in all things is synonymous with "God." We are about to begin to dig in to these teachings and we will be discussing evolution, but not just biological evolution as did Charles Darwin in his book *On the Origin of Species*.[23] We will look at biological evolution in a different context; through the lens of Esotericism.

Darwin was a naturalist writing about his findings in the natural world. He was intrigued by his observations of different types of sea turtles and finches that lived on the different islands of the Galapagos chain. They were each suited particularly to the island on which they lived and it's terrain. He wondered how that might come about through different natural processes and his conclusions on natural selection through random mutations were not very controversial when he released them. They actually numbered among many varied ideas posed by other scientists of his time. As usual, they were not immediately accepted.

---

[22] Reverend James Ussher was Archbishop of Armagh, and Primate of Ireland between 1625 and 1656. He published a chronology based on Biblical bloodlines that placed the date of creation as the night preceding Sunday, 23 October 4004 BC, according to the Julian calendar.

[23] Charles Darwin - *On the Origin of Species by means of natural selection* (London: John Murray Publishing 1859)

The idea of random evolution forwarded by Darwin had a chief competitor in its own time, in the theory as proposed by Jean Baptiste Lamarck. He believed that striving toward experience was the driving force in the evolutionary drama as it unfolds. In other words, the consciousness is what is important in the survival of the physical creature, and that individuals could affect the evolution of their species. The mind is the first tool of consciousness, and we can see the effect of evolution on the mind in the development of either a child, or a race, over eons. I obviously believe that physical evolution is the result of the evolution of consciousness as alluded to in our Fourth Key. This falls into harmony with the Lamarckian theory of evolution much more than the work of Darwin. This approach also takes away the accident of life argument, which counters the intuition and favors non evolutionary or *creationist* theory.

The modern work in the field of epigenetics is bringing us to a better understanding of how this internal evolution in the conscious observer affects and is evidenced in the physical world. Genes, which were once considered the only necessary indicator of everything from health to hair color, are now seen as potentials or predispositions that can be switched on or off through behavior. Yes, your behavior effects genetic expression, not exclusively the reverse. Although those influences are easy to infer from family likeness and body types, it is unclear where nature ends and nurture takes over.

It is easy to recognize cause and effect in some situations but be careful about what you assume, always. Lifestyle choices create the environment that is either favorable or unfavorable for the expression of dis-ease. In a study of breast cancer patients, the mutation of the BRCA1 and BRCA2 genes identified as the "cause" by allopathic medicine, actually accounts for less than 10% of the cases.[24] The top five risk factors are all lifestyle based. They include the usual suspects; cigarette smoking, obesity and stress, all evidenced as more important than the gene itself. Thus the survival of the body is much less dependent on the body's own make up than the behavior of the conscious living entity who is inhabiting

---

[24] Susan G. Komen – Genetics and Breast Cancer Fact Sheet.

it and in effect, driving. If it is balanced in its approach to the physical emotional and mental nature, the lower self will be well-adjusted and make decisions that are true to the interest of the whole. Over emphasis on any one of these aspects of the personality will thwart the expression of the others and this imbalance causes disease.

Evolution actually proceeds along three lines. The first and most obvious is physical, which we easily recognize as the changing of the form or outer appearance. The next is psychic evolution, referring to Soul or consciousness (they are synonyms). There are, as a result of this evolution, many differing levels of consciousness and we will explore some of them together as we proceed. This aspect of evolution will occupy us more than either of the other two. The last is spiritual evolution. This is the evolution of the spiritual essence itself; the driving force or energy and the One Life within whom we live and move and have our being. Yes, I just said *God* evolves, as does everything else. My uncle Ed O'Connor once said that "Evolution is the process of God becoming aware of itself." This is a brilliant idea that I believe warrants consideration. As I said, psychic evolution will occupy most of our time but we must begin at the beginning and for me that means defining the field of play, or the environment in which all of this occurs. Let's go back to some of the symbolism that has been used to describe, on many different levels, the process of creation.

The universe is the field of play in all of its different phases of evolution and manifestation. It is that which truly embraces us on our journey and incidentally, evolves with us because it *is* us. The universe is a living, evolving organism of which you are a fragment. It has been symbolized by the unbroken circle throughout the ages. This is perhaps because the circle has no beginning and no end. It does however cause a contradiction in one way. It seems to be circumscribed with a barrier or as the teachings say, a "ring pass not." This is not accurate in any strict sense. The universe is infinite but it does contain many *systems* which do have effective or practical barriers. As self-conscious entities we have the ability to push back that ring pass not and expand our awareness.

29

On September 12, 2013 NASA announced that the Voyager probe was the first manmade object to actually leave the solar system. It travelled over 11 billion miles over the course of 36 years to escape the gravitational influence of the sun, which defines this imaginary barrier. Man is many years away from having this experience for himself, although as we peer deep into space with our ever more powerful telescopes we are in a sense, looking back in time. The distances are so great that the images we see represent events that occurred, in some cases, billions of years ago because of the time it takes light to travel such vast distances. Let's see if we can get a grasp on the idea of the infinite universe. How do you imagine something large enough that you could travel billions of years at the speed of light and still not get across? Turn on your creative imagination.

As a thought experiment, let's try for a moment to imagine a universe that is not infinite. It might be easier to frame this way, as we did with the concept of esotericism itself. If the universe is finite it has to be measurable. That is what finite means. In order to measure something we must have a point of reference and it is very helpful if not absolutely necessary, that the reference point be outside the system. It is really difficult to measure the size of a forest from the middle, or for that matter any place inside the forest unless you know exactly where you are, in which case the forest has already been measured and mapped. Ideally we would want to start our measurement from the edge or beginning. That means we would be supposing a place where you could erect a barrier or first point to measure from. Ponder for a moment the idea that the ability to see the universe from its edge places the observer outside of it.

No matter where we decided to erect it, this imaginary barrier would divide the universe against itself. When we divide it with this barrier we are confronted with the obvious question; what is on the other side of the barrier? No matter how far out we went there would always be more empty space on the other side of our measuring point. If you think about it you cannot ignore empty space because the universe, just like matter, is almost entirely empty space. HPB said the universe "has its center everywhere and its circumference nowhere." By this definition you are now at the center of the universe and you are reading a book there... nice.

For practical purposes, we do have to consider the content of that universe. It exists in varying phases of energy which manifest (as we shall see later on) as a result of consciousness. These are phases and levels of energetic matter, one within the other. The inner energy literally creates the substance of the outer form and that in turn, creates the next more dense and limited form, in many successive *octaves* of vibration. As we discussed earlier, we are going to simplify it for the moment to two phases coexisting, one within the other. We will explore the many gradations of this energetic matter in our discussion of the Seven Planes of Manifestation in Chapter 13. For the moment we will refer to the two as the obstructed and unobstructed "phases" of the one universe.[25]

These are the physical manifestation in the obstructed phase and the underlying cause in the unobstructed or un-manifested (metaphysical) phase. Remember what Einstein told us with his laws of conservation - that matter and energy are merely two interchangeable states of the same essence. Neither can be created or destroyed, but merely converted into its other native phase.

If we begin with the unobstructed, we must rely on our definition of esoteric as a guide, because it is difficult to discuss something that isn't. In the unobstructed universe time and space do not exist. They would have to be considered obstructions. Distance, or the time it takes to cross a given distance, creates a temporal barrier to travel or communication, even if there are no physical obstructions. The unobstructed is infinite and un-manifested. It is indefinable for us at this level of consciousness, for consciousness requires form. It is the spiritual realm that underlies all manifestation. It is self-sustaining and self-existent, and it is the cause of the physical world.

At this moment 100 billion sub atomic particles called neutrinos are screaming through every square centimeter of your body every second.[26]

---

[25] This idea is built up in detail in the book *The Unobstructed Universe* by Stuart Edward White. (New York: E.P. Dutton and Company, Inc, 1940)

[26] Brian Cox and Jeff Forshaw – *Why does E=mc2 (and Why Should we Care?)* (Philidelphia: De Capo Press 2009)

They are unimpeded and unnoticed because they do not interact with the matter of your body in the physical or obstructed universe. Now these neutrinos are actually physical matter, but they are not obstructed by the matter of our bodies, or the earth, so I hope it gives the sense of what I am trying to convey. This is the zero point field of quantum theory; pure un-manifested potential.

Quantum theory refers to a phenomenon known as wave-particle duality. When a photon is traveling it behaves as a wave. It is conducted through the environment and coalesces as material only when it impacts and so interacts with matter, or is observed. In motion, it is like a wave that is conducted through the medium of the ocean, traveling as a potential alone without taking the water with it. Movement of the water along a certain path is considered a current. A fishing bobber on the surface gives way to the wave and is moved in a vertical ellipse returning to roughly the same position after the wave has passed. The wave moves through the medium of the water as a pure potential that is only realized when it impacts something such as a dock, or the shoreline itself, at which point we can see immense power manifested. Light is conducted through the environment in much the same way. Empty space is not empty. It conducts light and mind, and it is filled with the fabric of all of the conflicting gravitational and electromagnetic influences. Consciousness moves like this as well.

Next we have the obstructed phase - the exoteric manifested "reality" that we all share and yet, interpret for ourselves in many different ways. We live in this obstructed phase, or at least those aspects of ourselves with which we seem most deeply identified live here. This is where duality reigns and we have time and space and other physical manifestations as obstructions. Every front has a back and every top has a bottom. Everything including motion itself must be measured in its relationship to something else. It is a very limiting form of existence. This is the one reality science (outside of quantum theory) recognizes as the only universe. Not only does the unobstructed universe exist, but the obstructed is actually dependent on it and built on the *scaffolding of energy* in the unobstructed phase.

At this point I need to formally introduce the first of our seven keys as a hypothesis, and give you an indication of the depth of this idea: Remember, we are taking a scientific look at spiritual principles, and this technically does not fit that definition for reasons stated above. For our purposes, this is a working theory that will show itself repeatedly throughout our conversations as a reasonable assumption on which to base further exploration. It happens to be the first of three overriding principles at the core of our seven keys. As in all manifestation, the trinity gives birth to the septinate. Three is the number of creation and seven the number of manifestation.

The universe is permeated by and completely immersed in this single source of energy. A single unifying energy that is the underlying cause of all that is, and all that is not. It has been called *the ultimate abstraction* by philosophy, the quantum or *zero point field* by science, and of course *God* by the religions of the world. The Esoteric Scientist (or at least this one) simply refers to it as "Life."

The word God has too much baggage and misunderstood symbolism attached to it. I think life, or even, "the force" as it was referred to in the Star Wars series, is a more accurate, or at least a less charged term. If you take any prayer or scripture and replace the word God wherever it is used with the words life or life force, the thoughts conveyed still work, and sometimes work better. I will be using the word God as well, but I consider the terms to be interchangeable in a practical sense.

There are some ramifications to the use of this as a working hypothesis. It intimates that everything in the universe is alive. Even what has been referred to as dead matter is permeated by this life force. Nothing is dead. We can divide it into organic when the life is evident and inorganic when it is not, but it is all alive. It is all a manifested or material state that a living force is using to express, experience, and evolve through. This is the basis of the belief of Hylozoism and is closely related to Pantheism. (see keys one, two and four)

The One Life, or this life force, is the source of all being. This is the justification of the idea behind unity of being or the religious idea of brotherhood. We must not limit this to just human life but all life. This is also the reason for the idea that separation is an illusion. You and me and the space between us are united by this spiritual energy. The New Testament put this idea into two different concepts that are reflections of each other. St. Paul said God is "through all, above all, and in you all" (Eph 4:6). This is what is termed *God Immanent*. God (Life) is in all things. In the book of Acts we read that God is "He in whom we live and move and have our being" (Acts 17:28). This is the concept of *God Transcendent*, which is focused upon by most religious people. God is something outside of, and greater than the self, and envelops it. Ask yourself, what part of creation lies outside of God? What part of God could be considered dead? You may see this coming, but I believe both God Transcendent and God Immanent are true and useful ideas.

If God is in all, and all is in God, what causes the differences? Why are rocks different from people? How is it that this universal essence permeates all things and yet seems to produce something different each time, and in every case a unique form? We are going to be looking at this force in many different ways so we may as well start here. This force expresses itself through three major aspects in varying degrees. We will get much deeper into these ideas later on, but they are important to consider and keep in mind as we proceed. They are:

Will – The driving force. This is the urge that sets everything into motion. It drives the flower out of the ground and is the creator behind all manifestation. It also drives me to teach and express in every way that I do. The "Will of God" is the impetus of physical creation. Andrew Cohen refers to this as the evolutionary impulse in his work *Evolutionary Enlightenment*.[27]

Love or Love/Wisdom – This is not the love we feel for a wife or child. That is an expression on a lower level of this universal law. It is the quality of attraction and repulsion on every level of existence. It is the binding force of the universe. It holds the electron in the orbit of the atom, and

---

[27] Andrew Cohen – Evolutionary Enlightenment (New York: Select Books; 1ST edition 2011)

the earth in the orbit of the sun. It holds my body together. Will provides the impetus; Love is the cohesive agent which provides the form.

Activity – or more appropriately, **Intelligent Activity**. It manifests as adaptability in nature. It is Active Intelligence or mind at work. This is the order of the universe. We may not be able to perceive it with our human consciousness but it is everywhere. Animals are intelligent. Chemicals discriminate. This is the order behind natural selection. Mind is the organizing force of creation and it permeates the pre-existent matter of the universe.

Thus we have what is religiously characterized as "The Will of God, the Love of God, and the Mind of God." Three potentials expressed by this singular life force in the act of creation. For Moses, God was an all-consuming fire. This fire is the essence of all things. It is the basis for the violent fission going on in the furnace of the sun, and the metabolism of your body, which believe it or not, by mass, is a more efficient generator of energy than the sun.[28]

We are going to look at the smallest spark of that fire. If it's everywhere and it is the "essence of all," I should be able to look at a fragment of it and understand it like I would with the ocean, or your blood. This individual spark is sometimes referred to as the Monad, and that concept is often attributed to Gottfried Leibniz, but it actually has its origin in the work of Pythagoras. Its parallel in modern physics is the "quanta" of Max Plank. He theorized that all could be reduced to these individual energy packets he called quanta, and that they are the ground of all manifested being. All is energy. We will now take a look at one possible model of the life experience of one of these little sparks.

---

[28]   Cox and Forshaw – Why Does E=MC2 and Why Should We Care

The Parable of Alphie

For our discussion we will borrow from my father's first book, *Echoes From Eternity*[29] and call our little spark or Monad "Alphie." For a more in depth look at this principle please refer there. We will look at one possible model of how Alphie evolves through a cyclic process called metempsychosis, or what is scripturally referred to as the transmigration of Soul. I did propose earlier that not only consciousness and form evolve but that the spiritual essence evolves as well, and this will give us an idea of how that happens.

Like all else in the universe, Alphie vibrates. This means he has a frequency, or more accurately a frequency signature; a complex set of vibrations like a musical chord. Our Third Key tells us that all manifestation is based on this frequency. This is the second of the three overriding principles I mentioned. As he is able to increase or change the level of this vibration he will manifest in different ways. The difference between blue light and red light is nothing more than a variance of frequency within the band of electromagnetic radiation that we call visible light.

Let's say for argument's sake that he is starting at a low vibratory frequency. Based on his frequency he has a vibratory "affinity" for other like particles. This causes an attraction between them, and together they form a manifestation that is greater than any one of them. This a principle we will be seeing in manifestation throughout all of the levels of consciousness we explore and can be expressed in the wording of our Sixth Key "All forms of life embrace lesser forms and are in turn embraced by greater forms." This is the third principle at the core of the Seven Keys. Together, they state simply that there is One Life at the center of all being manifesting as the many, through the cyclic power of vibratory interaction, creating ever more complex expressions of life, within life, all within the One.

---

[29]   Anthony J. Fisichella - *Echoes From Eternity* (USA: Authorhouse 2004) www. authorhouse.com - Originally published by Llewellyn Books 1984 under the title *Metaphysics: The Science of Life.*

Before we go any further we need to address resonance and dissonance, or the idea of affinity. Resonance or affinity based on vibration is what causes us discomfort in the presence of a certain person or place and comfort in another. It's not good or bad it is just resonance or dissonance, like musical notes that don't go together. Colors can do the same thing. They can clash and cause us to withdraw or blend well, and put us at ease. When we wear colors that don't "go together" we are a walking clash of energies.

Electrical particles with affinity for each other can together, produce an atom. In our case let's say that Alphie and others with whom he has this affinity produce a hydrogen atom. He is vibrating at low frequency and produces a simple or low level of manifestation. Hydrogen is the simplest atom and thus the simplest material manifestation. It has just one proton, one neutron, and one electron. For the sake of clarity, let me say that I am not claiming that hydrogen has a particular frequency, but chose it for its simplicity.

Life is an infinite spectrum of vibrations. Light, sound and heat are sections or "frequency bands" within that spectrum. Mineral "life" is at a very low part of the spectrum but forms the substance inhabited by conscious entities of a higher form, and benefits through this interaction. This is a part of the Law of Redemption. Alphie, as a part of this manifestation, is a prisoner until the hydrogen atom is ignited and thus destroyed. Then he is back in the unobstructed universe. Matter has been converted into energy. Once out of manifestation he is different now, having had the experience of existence in the physical world. He will cycle in and out of manifestation over and over again; taking form in the obstructed universe, and then processing in the unobstructed, the experience he has gained in the form, raising his vibratory frequency as he goes.

This leads us into another idea with regard to the evolutionary process. Throughout all of these cycles we are dealing essentially with two types of evolution. The first is qualitative evolution, and represents fixed potential. It is determined by the level of vibratory frequency as the energy in question enters into manifestation. The other is quantitative evolution and represents the amount of that potential that is realized. Let's look at these ideas within a specific context and I will show you what I mean.

As a human being, each of us has a certain potential for mental acuity. That is, for all practical purposes, set. It is your mental capacity, and in this context the word *capacity* is perfect. If your IQ is 145 or higher you are considered a genius, but does that guarantee you will become an accomplished mathematician or inventor? Obviously not. That capacity is like a cup. You can fill it to the brim, but you can't get a bigger cup. The IQ is a gift, like any other talent and if you apply it and use it, you gain experience you would not otherwise gain. You can choose activities that bring out your strengths and *realize* your potential, or not. You can use that potential for the good of all, or become a really effective con man or criminal. You may lie around and not really *become* at all.

Being a musician makes you look at the world differently. If you have a gift for music and never use it, you will not experience the change of perspective that comes with the development of musical talent. If you do develop it, you will have more to work with and gain a better understanding, even in the supposedly unrelated areas of your life. Exposing children to music helps them with pattern recognition and mathematics.

Back to Alphie – When the hydrogen was burned he entered the unobstructed universe and his frequency began to charge up. The experience of having been in manifestation will be pored over in the pralaya or rest period in between manifestations. (This is when you get a bigger cup.) The Monad is not frozen in a form and can change.

In human expression this translates into the cycles of incarnation. Your potential for interaction is increased by the degree to which you perfect the control of your mechanism. In the next cycle you will have to relearn everything, including walking and talking, but you will learn some things better and faster and you will have certain talents that reflect your past experiences and what you learned from them. You build a better form because your capacities have increased. Have you ever experienced a relationship that felt like a trap? After leaving a situation like that, we often realize a growth in awareness and change in attitudes.

OK, now let's bring in the Fifth Key that will guide us on our way. "As it is above, so it is below." It is reflected in a more modern phrase you may not have been exposed to. *Ontogeny recapitulates Phylogeny*. This is also recognized in the phrase *man is made in God's image*. It supposes that what I can say of the microcosm, I can presume in the macrocosm and is a simplistic statement of the Law of Correspondences.

Science is not quite there yet. They still have not forged a unifying theory in which sub-atomic particles and large objects conform to the same laws, but they are definitely looking. String theory and the idea of a 10 dimensional universe is giving way to the 11th dimension and the strings disappear into a membrane, ala "the fabric of the universe" or of "space/ time." And guess what? It's vibrating. Interestingly, this idea of vibrating strings coincides directly with what are known as spirulae as they are described by the Tibetan Master Djwahl Kuhl in *A Treatise on Cosmic Fire*.[30]

As evolution proceeds we will come to a point where the vibration is so great that the particles themselves break up, as in radio activity. This can be seen as "self-destruction" or as an entrance into a higher plane of manifestation. Alphie will eventually reach a point in his development when he can no longer find meaningful expression in the Mineral Kingdom alone. His vibration has become so high that he requires a more appropriate form of life within which to express himself, and along with others who have reached this stage, he moves into the Plant Kingdom. Now, he is still manifesting as part of an atom that is now a part of something greater. Plants are mineral life on a higher turn of the evolutionary spiral. The Plant Kingdom literally builds itself of and emerges from the Mineral Kingdom.

Life in the Mineral Kingdom focuses on Intelligent Activity or adaptability. As hard as that may be to accept, minerals do grow in an organized fashion, and chemicals will interact in a predictable and repeatable manner. Thus each exhibits a rudimentary form of mind, if

---

[30]   Alice A Bailey - *A Treatise on Cosmic Fire* (New York: Lucis Publishing Company 1925)

mind is to be held as an organizing force. In this new form of expression the focus is on Love or sentient responsiveness. Plants respond to love. Anyone who is a plant person can tell you this is true. A scientist named Cleve Backster did experiments with polygraphs in the 1960s and 70's proving environmental awareness in plants which we will discuss further on. It is worth googling him. (It's hard to believe "googling" is a real word but here we are in the 21st century.)

When Alphie is in the plant he is a prisoner again. It is mineral life at a higher level of expression but he is locked in a form. He is released into the unobstructed universe when the plant is eaten or dies and de-composes. Once again, his exposure to this higher form of consciousness enhances his growth and forwards the evolutionary process. If the plant is eaten and converted into energy Alphie is now free again in the unobstructed universe. This repeats over and over through the course of eons.

Again a point is reached in which Alphie cannot grow in awareness and expression within the Plant Kingdom, and a transformation takes place bringing him into manifestation in the Animal Kingdom. Is Alphie now an animal? No. He wasn't a plant or a mineral either. He is joining together with all of the other little life entities with which he has affinities to create a form, and cycling endlessly, always being affected by these different relations.

The focus is now on Will. Animals express a very definite Will, and also reason. They have objective awareness but not subjective awareness. In other words while they have reason they do not have self-consciousness. Even this barrier is being blurred by the interaction of the Animal Kingdom with humanity. I have seen individuation of varying degrees in so called domesticated animals but sooner or later a change will come and Alphie will be ready to enter the Human Kingdom.

Before we take that step, let me say one more thing in this regard. All of the matter that makes up the various bodies of a human being are composed of Monads. Alphie, as a part of a plant, made up of minerals may have been ingested by an animal or human being and become part of the muscle tissue as a part of a cell. At the time of the death of the cell he is flushed from the body and again decomposes and is turned back into energy. The exposure to the higher levels of consciousness raises his vibrations. Consciousness affects the material from which it builds its form and all along, Alphie has simply been a part of that form.

We are about to consider an enormous change here. Alphie can no longer find value in the expressions available within the vehicle whether that is a flower, a horse or a human. He may have been a part of a human form (a sophisticated animal body) and garnered that experience but now he is so evolved he needs a complete form for his own use. He has been affected by every form he has participated in creating. Alphie now must take the next step in the evolution of his awareness and build a form for his now individualized expression. He is inherently self-conscious and his new task is to express the "I Am" in form.

We are now in the human Kingdom and we have come full circle through all of the aspects of the Trinity. Now the focus is back on Intelligent Activity. Will, Love, and Intelligent Activity are in higher expression than ever before but as before one is dominant, like the dominant note in a chord that lends it more color than any of the other sub-tones.

Alphie has been initiated into the Human Kingdom and goes through a process we will deal with in greater detail in Chapter 6 on the anatomy of consciousness. He is now a Human Monad and the process of Metempsychosis is re classified as re-incarnation. (In the flesh) The Human Monad is "like unto the father in terms of Godhood, but not like unto the father in terms of manhood."[31] Think in terms of a child and a man. One is less developed but they are equally human. Evolution will take Alphie beyond human expression as well. If this entire progression could be stated in a single sentence it would be the well-known Kabalistic saying referenced in The Secret Doctrine; "The Breath becomes a stone; the stone, a plant; the plant, an animal; the animal, a man; the man, a spirit; and the spirit, a God." In an interview published in The Scientific

---

[31] Anthony Fisichella – *The Well of Wisdom* audio course on metaphysics. (Higher Ground Publishing 2004)

American,[32] Thomas Edison makes a number of statements which embrace this idea and state it so simply that a few of them are worth repeating here.

> *Life, like matter is indestructible.*

> *Our bodies are composed of myriads of infinitesimal entities, each in itself a unit of life; just as the atom is composed of myriads of electrons.*

> *The human being acts as an assemblage rather than as a unit; the body and mind express the vote or voice of the life entities.*

> *The life entities build according to a plan. If a part of the life organism be mutilated, they rebuild exactly as before ......*

> *Science admits the difficulty of drawing the line between the inanimate and the animate; perhaps the life entities extend their activities to crystals and chemicals ......*

> *The life entities live forever; so that to this extent at least the eternal life which many of us hope for is a reality.*

The Hierarchy of Conscious Evolution

Let's take a close look at what is happening to Alphie subjectively. Alphie is a unit of sentient energy moving in and out of form. In accordance with the Law of Correspondences and our Fifth Key, I would like to postulate what is happening to him. The model I am using for this example comes from the book *Cosmic Consciousness* by Richard Maurice Bucke.[33] Alphie is under a constant barrage of energies which all act as stimuli coming from his environment. In the Mineral and Plant Kingdoms he has no

---

[32] Harper's Magazine for February, 1890, and which is enlarged upon in the Scientific American for October, 1920.

[33] Richard Maurice Bucke - *Cosmic Consciousness: A Study in the Evolution of the Human Mind* (Detroit: Wayne State University Press, 1977)

objective awareness we can speak of, although we know he interacts with his environment never-the-less. Percepts or "sense impressions" impact the infant consciousness. He registers nothing at first.

I'll give you a practical physical plane example (as above so below). An amoeba is stimulated by a scientist through changes in light, sound and temperature etc. It responds without knowing where the stimulus is coming from or even that it is responding. It moves towards or away from stimuli based on affinity with no subjective awareness of like or dislike. As these sense impressions aggregate they become something to which Alphie can respond. Together they form a "recept." In concert with each other they finally become something that means something. Rather than moving away because the environment is changing he is sensing food for example, and can take appropriate action. There is still no subjective awareness but we can see that there is a change. The environmental data has been aggregated and assessed.

The electron gun in the cathode ray tube of an old TV creates lines with dots until an image is formed. Only together do they assemble a picture. If you get too close or try to concentrate your awareness on individual dots you will lose the image. This idea was actually developed by a farmer who realized he could draw a picture in his field as he plowed it by dropping and raising the blade of his plow.[34] Corn Mazes are pictures drawn in the rows of corn by removing parts of the matrix.

The receptual mind has objectivity and can respond to images as well as create them. Recepts aggregate in a similar manner until a concept is formed. This new and complete idea is filed away in the memory under a label or tag, which is a very important leap. This is the start of… language. Now we have the <u>conceptual or human mind</u>. Alphie is now a Human Monad.

Words are symbols that do not look like the objects they symbolize. They are like mathematical formulae for ideas. Think of a school kid

---

[34]   I was unable to verify this legend given to me by my 12th grade electronics teacher Carmine Farinola but I liked it as much as I liked Mr. Farinola and so, used it here.

adding long columns of numbers in comparison to a mathematician who can do the same work with a powerful, yet simple formula. Man only had to invent each tool once and then could recognize situations where it can be used, modified or reapplied. Let's look at the concept of concepts with a simple one we all recognize, the automobile.

To the layman this represents a mode of transportation - a wheeled vehicle with a steering mechanism and a motor. You put in the key, and it goes. Cars became subtle statements of style over time because of the manipulations of advertising, but we all pretty much look at a car and its utility in the same way.

To the Engineer we have an added set of symbols. He will immediately think in terms of the mechanics. He might think of crankshafts, pistons and other aspects of internal combustion engines in addition to what the layman thought. He might think in terms of the evolution of suspension systems that improved the performance over decades, rather than the sporty air foil the designer used to make people want it. The concept is a variable and will mean different things to different people based on their background. This may seem unimportant at first but the implications of conceptual awareness are staggering. The ability to conceptualize implies self-awareness. The conceptual mind is capable of subjectivity. It can assert "I am," and further, "I am responding to X." The conscious entity is now aware of being aware and capable of using the mind to alter behavior based on the recognition of patterns emerging in the environment.

If I am at home with my dog Queenie and we both see the door to the house, we both know it's there and how it works. If it's closed, neither of us will smack into it and if the dog wants out and can't operate the handle, she will scratch on it in a frustrated attempt to get through. I have seen video of dogs and cats alike that could operate the door, and even colluded in the effort, but there is a difference. I know that I know it and she does not. I can step aside myself and examine my own internal state of being; the working of my mind, the effects of my emotional nature etc. This is true *self consciousness*.

This stage of awakening is symbolized in the Garden of Eden. Animal man becomes self-aware, gets dressed and starts to work. The need for privacy or the feeling of exposure at being unclothed is a statement of awareness of the self and a consequent need for boundaries. This sense of self grants humanity the capacity to create beauty, music and art - either for the sense of personal accomplishment, or in order to bring something extraordinary into the lives of those around us. The musician or artist tries to convey what he feels through his creation as he is creating but there is a flip side. The sense of self is the gift/curse of human consciousness. I can feel bad about myself if my car or house isn't as nice as my neighbor's. We can sometimes express ourselves to the detriment of our fellow human beings. The focus of all of our energy on the personal self can be detrimental and create greed and hate. The need for a harmless attitude, as taught by the Masters, becomes more understandable under these conditions.

Percepts, recepts and concepts are continuing to aggregate and we will find over time that we, as a species, will develop awareness of things that today completely escape our conscious recognition. If we go back in time far enough there is no reference in ancient texts to fragrance or color. It is possible the writings precede the development of those senses. We are now on the verge of etheric vision and some of us already have it. Psychic sensitivities are another example of this, but the next major step is into the realm of the higher Intuition. This is not the so called *gut feeling* we share with the Animal Kingdom.

The true intuition grants the ability to apprehend truth without a reasoning process. It requires no logic to reflect truth. This is sometimes called "Cosmic Consciousness" but that is a bit of a misnomer because you don't have the understanding of the entire cosmos or universe. Group consciousness or soul consciousness may be closer. The Monad moves from consciousness of the self to consciousness of the group in which it is an integral part. Think about what would happen if all of your cells suddenly became aware (at least in part) of your greater purpose. Imagine what that would do to you. This is analogous to all of humanity becoming aware of the grand purpose of humanity as a whole. Imagine what the world would be like if we all became aware of the evolutionary plan and began to work in harmony with it consciously.

It would lead us collectively into the Fifth Kingdom of Nature. We would all become initiated into the mysteries and evolution would be accelerated in a manner that is unimaginable. We would all become Christ like in our awareness but is that as far as it goes? I don't think so. We can see consciousness on many levels, whether we can accept the idea of mineral consciousness or not. I don't think there are too many of us who would deny it in a plant. We see it accelerated through the Animal Kingdom and reaching incredible heights in man. Why would we assume it has climbed to its limit, or the idea that there is a limit at all?

CHAPTER 5

Reincarnation And Karma

We have posited the existence of one all-pervasive force in the universe and the idea that this force exists within and between all things, unobstructed and unimpeded. We have discussed how this justifies, to an extent, the concept of unity within all existence that is the basis of our First Key. We have further offered the idea that this root principle or spiritual energy is cycling in and out of manifestation, and that consciousness is expanding into greater self-awareness through this process, called metempsychosis. Now we are going to explore the process of metempsychosis as it relates to the human consciousness, where it is termed reincarnation. We will see the effects which are described in Keys Two through Four and governed by the Law of Cyclic Activity.

Reincarnation and Karma are both widely misunderstood, like so many other topics in spirituality or religious doctrine. Rebirth is a controversial concept, because of its connection to religion and our understanding of life and death itself. If we are going to understand these things we need to start with an understanding of what makes up a human being. This is one of the instances where we need only start with a sketch of an idea in order to understand a related subject. Later we will add color and depth to this construct once we have, in this case, established an understanding of the cycles through which it passes.

We can all attest to the fact of the physical body and most of us believe there is an indwelling Soul which is our essence. For the time being, we are considering Monad and Soul to be synonymous terms relating to the spiritual essence at our core. We have an emotional nature as well, which can truly dominate the lives of many people. With effort we can learn to stand aside our emotions and examine them. As much as it may seem like this is the real you, it is not. You are the observer, not the observed. You have a mind but that can also be examined by the real you - the consciousness itself that makes you who you are. We are all similar physically and what makes us look different is a small fraction of what we share, even on the level of the physical body and its intricate workings. However, each of us as a consciousness is quite unique. You are in part the product of your experiences. Your third grade teacher had an impact on you. Perhaps you can't identify it specifically, but it's there. I'm going to give you another (qualified) hypothesis about how deep this theory goes.

The universe is the manifestation of one essence of all existing *life*. You are a spark of that life. Yours is the life of a Soul, which is divided from that universal essence only by a level of vibration, like an ice cube floating in the water that forms its totality. Floating separately because it has crystallized and its molecules are vibrating more slowly, and nothing else.

Any level of manifestation is the result of the frequency of its vibratory signature. Ice, water and steam are all identical on a molecular level but due to a variance in the frequency of the vibrations they are quite different in manifestation. A Monad's vibration is forged through its field of experience. It has unlimited potential and progresses in its ability to express more accurately that pure essence and perfection. This process is called evolution. And as we observe through our third key to the mysteries, it flows in cycles. The cycles of life surround us. The seasons, tides and everything else are tied to the solar and planetary cycles. The earth's rotation gives us our day and night and the moon's orbit gives us the month and the tides. Our year is determined by the earth's orbit around the sun. Could it be any other way?

So we have lives within lives and cycles as parts of greater cycles due to the constant rhythmic motion of the cosmos. Nothing is stagnant and all motion is relative. Worlds rotate and orbit each other. The pull of the gravitational fields and the radiation of electromagnetic and other energies form a cosmic dance of the heavenly bodies traveling through space. They are all interrelated, interconnected and manifesting as the simple cycles we perceive here on earth.

The Logos or God of our system is the Sun. It gives life through its radiation and keeps us within its aura with the gravity exerted by its very presence. Man is the God of his system and those lesser lives within the sphere of his influence. The human consciousness has many aspects to its nature and expresses this spiritual force on many levels. The Soul is a reflection of this force and then repeats the process, utilizing the personality as its vehicle. This too is a multi-layered expression with only the most dense and physical being obvious to the average man. There is an epic poem by Robert Browning called "A Death in the Desert" from which I have taken an excerpt. It describes this layered interaction better than I can hope to.

"Three souls which make up one soul; first, to wit,
A soul of each and all the bodily parts,
Seated therein, which works, and is what Does, And has the use of
earth, and ends the man Downward: but, tending upward for advice,
Grows into, and again is grown into
By the next soul, which, seated in the brain, Useth the first with
its collected use, And feeleth, thinketh, willeth, -- is what Knows
Which, duly tending upward in its turn,
Grows into, and again is grown into By the last soul, that uses both
the first, Subsisting whether they assist or no, And, constituting man's
self, is what Is – And leans upon the former, makes it play, As that
played off the first, and, tending up,
Holds, is upheld by, God, and ends the man Upward in that dread
point of intercourse, Nor needs a place, for it returns to Him.
What Does, what Knows, what Is; three souls, one man."

What "Does" is the human personality or animal soul. What "Knows" is the reincarnating Ego or Human Soul. What "Is" is the Monad clothed as the Solar Angel or Spiritual Triad.

Reincarnation in Religion

Let's take a look at this concept of reincarnation in the context of some of the major religious systems developed throughout the ages. We are going to start as far back as is practical, and move up into the modern age. Now, I did warn against authoritarian teaching, and in seeming contradiction to that idea I am about to begin quoting various religious writings. My purpose is not to say that this should be taken as truth because it exists in certain teachings but to show you that the idea is not as far *out there* as it may have been characterized. This doctrine of the transmigration of the human Soul is not just some new idea dreamed up in the 1960's by a bunch of pot smoking hippies. It has permeated the teachings of the ages and only recently has it been disregarded by some, even though it is expressed in the ancient scriptures of their own faith.

Hinduism is the faith of over a billion people. One of its central texts is called the Bhagavad Gita. It is actually a small part of an enormous text called the Mahabharata and translates as "The Song Celestial." In it Arjuna, a chariot warrior, is counseled by Krishna, the chariot driver and his spiritual guide. This is an allegory for the lower and higher aspects of one human being, the reader. Interestingly they both ride together on the physical frame, the chariot, which in accordance with Esoteric Buddhism is not considered a *principle* and has but a passive role, as a vehicle for both the lower and higher principles of consciousness in the human being. In this beautiful passage Krishna explains the immortality of the Soul and the cycles of incarnation it passes through as clothing to be discarded when it is worn out.

> *"I myself never was not, nor thou, nor all the princes of the earth. Nor shall we ever hereafter cease to be. As the lord of this mortal frame, experienceth therin infancy, youth, and*

*old age, so in future incarnations will it meet the same. One
who is confirmed in this belief is not dismayed by anything
that may come to pass. As a man throweth away old garments
and putteh on new, even so the dweller in the body having
quitteth its old mortal frames entereth into others that
are new."*

This is far from subtle. And it is perhaps less surprising than some of
the other quotes we will come to because of its source. This next passage
comes from the Taoist, Lao Tsu and is contained in a writing called the
Hua Hu Ching. In it a student inquires of his Master of whether some
of the aspects of man pass with him into his next incarnation, and why.

*Venerable Teacher, when a person passes away does his
cognition pass with him in his future lives?*

*Kind Prince, the basic function and ability of cognition
continues its growth when a soul is reborn into the physical
world; however, the content of cognition is generally not
carried with the soul…. Except for the deep experience of*

*certain training that is strongly built and forged, knowledge
is stripped away because the storage of such information is
related to brain cells rather than to basic patterns and deep
instincts of life.*

*Can intuitional ability be passed on from one lifetime to
another?*

*Insight is not the content of knowledge. Because it is not in
the realm of intellect it continues whenever and wherever
the being exits.*

Now a quote from the Buddha and we will be done with the Eastern
religions with which most Westerners have only a vague knowledge.
You may find more surprises when we get to the ones we are supposedly
living by.

> *"I, Buddha who wept with all my brother's tears, whose heart was broken by a whole world's woe, laugh and am glad for there is liberty. Ho he ye who suffer, know that ye suffer from yourselves. The books say well my brothers, each man's life, the outcome of his former living is. The bygone wrongs bring forth sorrows and woes. The bygone right breeds bliss. That which ye sow, ye reap. See yonder fields, the sesame, was sesame, the corn, corn. The silence and the darkness knew. So, is a man's fate born. He cometh reaper of the things he sowed, sesame, corn, so much cast in past birth. And so much weed and poison stuff which mar him and the aching earth. If he shall labor rightly rooting these and planting wholesome seedlings where they grew, fruitful and fair and clean the ground shall be, and right the harvest due. Such is the law which moves to righteousness which none at last can turn aside or stay. The heart of it is love the end of it is peace and consummation sweet. Obey"*

The first of what are considered to be religions of the West to arise was the Hebrew faith, and its close brother Judaism. In the familiar Kabalistic phrase referenced earlier we read: *The breath becomes a stone; the stone, a plant; the plant, an animal; the animal, a man; the man, a spirit; and the spirit, a God.* Is there any other way to interpret this statement than the idea of some spiritual essence moving in and out of ever more complex forms of expression? To put it in an undeniable human context the Rabbi Simeon Ben Johai makes this statement in the Zohar:

> *"All souls are subject to the trials of transmigration and no men know the designs of the most high with regard to them. They know not how they are being at all times judged, before coming into this world and when they leave it. They do not know how many transformations and mysterious trials they must undergo. How many souls come to this world without returning to the palace of the divine King. The souls must re-enter the absolute substance from whence they emerged. But to accomplish this end they must develop all the perfections, the germ of which is planted in them and if they have not*

fulfilled this condition during one life, they must commence another, a third, and so forth until they have acquired the contrition which fits them for union with God."

I find this extraordinary because if you asked one hundred Jews whether reincarnation was ever a part of their faith, which relies on the ancient writings for its foundation in every other area, the number who would say no would likely be in the nineties and many would refuse to believe it even if confronted with this quote.

This next quote comes from Rabbi Menasseh Ben Israel (1604 – 1657). He lived in England and was so influential there, that his efforts led to the elimination of Oliver Cromwell's legal prohibition of Judaism in London, which had stood 350 years. The faith and dogma were well worn at the time of this writing so the idea that this particular doctrine was held only briefly in the early stages of the development of this deeply traditional system of faith and belief is easily dismissed.

"The belief or the doctrine of the transmigration of souls is a firm and infallible dogma accepted by the whole assemblage of our church with one accord. So that there is none to be found who would dare to deny it. Indeed there are a great number of sages in Israel who hold firm to this doctrine so that they made it a dogma, a fundamental point of our religion. We therefore are in duty bound to obey, and to accept this dogma with acclimation, as the truth of it has been incontestably demonstrated by the Zohar and all of the books of the Cabalists."

This comes from the Quran and while it can be considered more cryptic than the others the meaning is still plain to me.

Have you not considered those who went forth from their homes for fear of death, and they were thousands, then Allah said to them Die; again he gave them life. (Quran 2:243).

So, whatever form may be referenced, death is not considered the end of existence but a transition in every one of these cases.

We have covered almost everyone on earth with the exception of the Christians and we know for sure that they do not believe in a reincarnating Soul. The Church has taught that the supposedly immortal Soul comes into existence at conception and then goes to either heaven or hell for eternity at the time of death. It is interesting to note that even in this case, death is not a cessation of existence. It does however, deny participation in the cyclic nature of the rest of creation. How can this be? Can something immortal really come into existence at the moment of conception?

The New Testament does not mention reincarnation directly so, if reincarnation is the truth of the nature of life and death why didn't Jesus teach it? That is a reasonable question and I think I have a reasonable answer. Jesus was a member of a sect known as the Essenes, with a community in Galilee as well as another at Qumran. They were a body of highly spiritual and deeply devout Jews. The previous quote from the Zohar goes back almost as far as the days Jesus walked the earth and gives us an understanding of the principles held in these mystical, and dare I say occult groups.[35] Jesus didn't need to teach them about this, because they already accepted the idea. It needed no contradiction like the concepts he addressed in the beatitudes in his sermon on the mount. In that sermon he enumerates many false impressions with an updated and more compassionate stance in the same way. You have been told this, (an eye for an eye) but I say to you now, (turn the other cheek). This would have been the moment, had he seen the need, to tell his followers something along the lines of "You have been told of the migration of Souls into new bodies but I say to you lo, the Soul takes but one abode and be careful what you do or its eternal damnation for you."

Now you may be thinking that argument is a bit thin. Agreed, but there is more. Do you recall the story of the man who was said to be known to be born blind? Here is the quote.

---

[35] The word occult simply means hidden but has come to be misunderstood as something nefarious.

> *"And as Jesus passed by, he saw a man which was blind from his birth. And his Disciples asked him saying, 'Master who sinned, he or his parents that he was born blind?' Jesus answered, neither hath this man sinned, nor his parents: but that the works of God should be made manifest in him." (John 9: 1-3)*

Now, that question really only has one interpretation. And even though his response may seem vague on the issue of cause, there is no doubt that in his answer Jesus allows for the possibility that someone can sin before they are born; just not this man, or his parents. Jesus was not one to pass up a teachable moment and I can't imagine this Master, in conversation with his most gifted and devoted students, allowing something like that to pass. Why would he not take that opportunity to correct this basic mistake? There is more. When Jesus told them of coming changes, in seeming contradiction to the prophecies, they questioned him.

> *"And his disciples asking him saying why then say the scribes that Elijah must come first and Jesus answered and said unto them 'Elijah truly shall first come and restore all things, but I say unto you that Elijah is come already and they knew him not, and have done to him whatsoever they liked. Likewise shall also the son of man suffer of them.' Then the disciples under stood that he spake to them of John the Baptist." (Matt. 17:10)*

"Then the disciples understood he spake to them of John the Baptist." I don't sense any surprise in the statement. It seems the concept of transmigration was understood and the only new information provided was that John was Elijah's new form. So at least in this one definite case John the Baptist is confirmed by Jesus *in his own words* to be the reincarnation of the Prophet Elijah. It can still be argued that not everyone gets to do this, but there is no denying the recognition of an entity moving from one body to another through the process of a normal death and birth. Neither Elijah nor John are reported to have had miraculous births. I can invoke the same logic used above to assert as a possibility that if this transmigration were a rare occurrence, Jesus would have clarified that as well. So where did this idea go and why is it no longer an accepted tenet, embraced by the masses of Christianity?

One of the more vocal proponents for the preexistence of the Soul and it cyclic return to physical incarnation was a third century writer named Origen. In 553 a council was held in Constantinople by Emperor Justinian. In the words of Geoffrey Hodson, this was not an ecumenical council but a regional one, and "so without universal authority."[36] It was in the midst of a great rift and struggle between the Eastern and Western rites of the Church. The entire Eastern rite was assembled, but only 5 bishops from the West were in attendance. Pope Vigilius refused to attend, even though he was in Constantinople at the time. The council issued Origin as well as other early church fathers an anathema of 15 points including reincarnation and other teachings as heresies. Rome was not there, and most now disclaim the results but they leave the tenets in place. Origen was considered "one of the most prominent of all the church fathers with the possible exception of St Augustine." (Encyclopedia Britannica) St Gregory of Nisa called him "the prince of Christian learning in the third century." What did Origen have to say about this doctrine?

This quote comes in the context of an argument ongoing between Origen and Celsus, a skeptic on the matter. Here Origen cites philosophers with whom his thoughts are in agreement, who have evidently been referenced by his opponent in support of other positions. Some consider this a disqualification of the argument but I believe he was buttressing his belief with the unspoken endorsement of these others with whom Celsus has obviously agreed on other issues.

> *"Is it not more in conformity with reason that every soul for certain mysterious reasons (I speak now according to the opinion of Pythagoras and Plato and Empedocles, whom Celsus frequently names) is introduced into a body, and introduced according to its deserts, and former actions? Is it not rational that souls should be introduced into bodies in accordance with their merits and previous deeds, and that those who have used their bodies in doing the utmost possible good should have a*

---

[36] Geoffery Hodson - *The Hidden Wisdom of The Holy Bible* (Theosophical Publishing House 1993)

right to bodies endowed with qualities superior to the bodies of others? The soul which is immaterial and invisible in its nature exists in no material place without having a body. A body suited to the nature of that place. Accordingly, it at one time puts off one body which was necessary before, but which is no longer adequate in its changed state, and it exchanges it for a second. The soul has neither beginning nor end. Every soul comes into this world strengthened by the victories or weakened by the defeats of its previous life. Its place in this world as a vessel appointed to honor or dishonor is determined by its previous merits or demerits. Its work in this world in determines its place in the world that follows this one.

I have one more quote and then we will move on. It comes from St. Gregory (257-332 AD). He states "It is absolutely necessary that the soul be healed and purified. If this does not take place during its life on earth it must be accomplished in future lives." It does not get any clearer than that but there are many sources for further information and we don't want to accept anything based on authority.

The Process

Is there any evidence of such a cycling in and out of human form? Surely we should be able to find people who have had some recollection of this process and even if that will not be personal knowledge on our part, it can present us with an opportunity to verify or contradict this idea at some level if we are to look deeply enough. Of course with a question as readily apparent as this, we can be sure someone has already done so. Enter Dr. Ian Stevenson of the University of Virginia.

Dr. Stevenson devoted more than forty years to the scientific documentation of past life memories of children from all over the world. He has over 3000 cases in his files. Many people, including skeptics and scholars, agree that these cases offer the best evidence presented in support of the concept of reincarnation. Dr. Stevenson preferred to work with children because their entire lifetimes could more easily be verified than that of an adult. Thus, the testimony they gave of places their parents affirmed they had never been were more credible. His work is worth looking into for those who are interested. Some of the stories are quite remarkable including children naming and identifying their former spouses and children, as well as their favorite meals and other personal information. Some of the subjects were able to lead investigators to former residences and even places where money had been hidden.

One of the more interesting areas of Dr. Stevenson's work involved the correspondence of a birthmark on the child to the cause of death of the supposed former personality. In 43 of 49 cases where medical documentation was available, a correlation occurred between a birthmark on the child and an injury to the specific area of the body of the person whose life they claimed to remember. In some cases this injury was the cause of death of the recalled personality.

Again, argument can be found on either side of every subject and it is up to the individual to decide what rings a responsive chord in her consciousness. I mean only to breach the subject so that it can be realized that this idea is not so far from the beaten path, but we have digressed long enough.

Let's discuss the process itself for that is the only thing that is of moment anyway. If we are dealing with universal law we should be able to see it everywhere. That is what makes it universal. In order to fully understand reincarnation we must also introduce another idea, which in a great sense is the determining factor in the directions these cycles take and that is of course, Karma.

Karma

This is one of those Sanskrit words I warned you about that has no direct English correlation but loosely translates to *action* or *deed*. It is known as the Law of Cause and Effect and functions on all planes of manifested existence, so let's start with the easiest one, the physical. In

1666 Sir Isaac Newton defined a set of Laws of Inertia or "cause and effect." This represents Karma on the physical plane and is so reliable that the entirety of scientific research has been built upon its tenets. The laws of motion and physical science as he described them still hold true in all but the quantum world of particle physics, a world to which he had no access. His equations are the reason the announcer at a baseball game can tell you how far a home run went, even if the ball left the stadium and landed in the parking lot. Based on its size, weight, speed, and trajectory, they know exactly where it will land. The same mathematics are used to guide satellites and land a craft in an exact spot on the moon.

For every action there is indeed an equal and opposite reaction but not only on the physical plane. What we have to realize is that when we move from that physical plane to another more rarified form of energetic expression, we have a different set of apparent causes. The human personality functions on the three lowest sets of planes or, within the "three worlds of human evolution" (Djwahl Kuhl). These are the Physical, Emotional and Mental Planes, so for any thought, feeling, or action, including speech, there is a result on that plane and then a reverberation onto the lower (or outer) planes that are constructed of the material of the higher (or inner) planes. I am a thinking, feeling, acting, and speaking consciousness. On the Physical, Astral and Mental planes there is a result, or more accurately a constant stream of interrelated results, from every thought feeling and action. How can we assume anything else?

In every case the reaction will be equal in quality and intensity but opposite in direction. If I hit the wall, the wall effectively hits me back, with the exact same force. The bat and the ball feel the same impact. The bat wins the day because it is heavier, it is moving faster and incidentally, is still under the power of the batter. His effort and follow through have an effect on the movement and direction of the ball because they remain in contact for a period of time.

I could go through the whole biblical exercise with this idea as well, because scripture and fable are extant with ideas along these lines. What ye sow, ye reap. He who lives by the sword dies by the sword. Whatever a man thinketh in his heart, so is he. An eye for an eye; but don't take vengeance yourself. Nature will balance everything. Trust the process. The putting out of the second eye still causes Karma, on both the actor and the society on whose behalf he is acting. We are not directly responsible for each of the crimes in our cities, but we are responsible for our system of so called justice as a whole and the punishment it meets out. We are equally responsible for the conditions in which people are forced to live that sometimes result in criminal behavior.

It is important to remember that in its essence, the Karmic process is not punitive. It is completely impersonal. The ball is not being punished for getting in the way of the bat. It is a relationship that could be seen as mathematical before personal or punitive. A better way to think of it is in terms of a buildup of energy. An earthquake is a momentary event that is the result of an ongoing process that may have built up over centuries. Without knowledge of the forces building up over time, it is easy to misconstrue the nature of the event.

Karma governs response on emotional and mental levels as well and reflects the actions of individuals and groups alike. It concerns both the incarnation you are living and the ones you will live. As we organize into societies, we are forming groups at many levels and the things groups do cause reactions at group levels. Our families carry Karma as units. Our countries have identities and whether we act as a whole in order to accomplish the greater good, or our own selfish ends, we accrue Karmic consequences as a group. Americans carry the consequences of our government's actions when they are seen by the world as imperialistic and the same thing happens if they are altruistic. We as individuals are seen as part of the problem or the solution and we are. Government is a manifestation of the will of its people or their lack of will. In bringing this up with a local radio show host, he complained that "people don't get the government they want" and advised me to travel the world. I would love to travel the world but I did not say "want." That is desire and has more to do with cultural expression. I said it was a reflection of their will. This is a deeply significant occult truth worth pondering.

In considering the effects of Karma as we perceive them, it is difficult not to get caught in the idea that what we are talking about is retributive justice. Some think that if something is stolen from them they must have stolen something in another life, or this life. That is an over simplification and while that is sometimes useful in illustration, it is never really a good way of understanding something in its true essence.

We have all seen a friend or acquaintance that is beginning to slip. They are making bad decisions but refuse to look at what they are doing and it is getting worse. We see them as an accident waiting for a place to happen and when it does we are not surprised. Perhaps you could not tell what was going to happen but you knew something had to give sooner or later. That is the turning of the Karmic wheel. Every act is instantly ennobling or detrimental but the results are not obvious or immediately apparent, most of the time. The ball doesn't know about the bat. It is just being a ball and the course it is traveling upon is altered by the bat, through the impersonal physical laws that represent the field of play. In this instance, we also have to consider the imposition of the will of the pitcher and then subsequently, the batter.

So, governed by law on all planes of manifestation, we have the cyclic return to form. In the human being we refer to this shedding of bodies with the term reincarnation. It is the cyclic return of the Ego or Soul into a sequence of garments, which it uses for the expression and advancement of its consciousness. Access to a part of that consciousness is lost while in form and the goal over time is to perfect the ability to remain conscious while in form, making more complete use of these different vehicles. People wonder "How many lives will I have?" The simple answer is you have just one life, with many episodes, or incarnations. In essence even this is an illusion and you are but a fragment of the One Life finding expression through all form. A Chinese woman and an American man in manifestation are the result of one consciousness taking in differing experience simultaneously, through more than one means of expression. You look different to those in your environment, but so do they and you may be following each other through many of these episodes.

Your five year old body was quite different than the one you have now and not a single cell remains of that previous form. Every seven to ten years you have a completely different body. Every cell is replaced in that period and some are replaced hundreds or thousands of times over. The "you" that is you is consistent through your growth and the physical changes, just as it is through all of those larger cycles and it shapes them. It gains in awareness of itself through this process in ever denser forms and planes of manifestation, until it has full awareness and Mastery while in incarnation.

The Soul

Most of the religious teachings of the world posit the existence of a Soul or inner being that inhabits the physical body. The Soul (the real you) has no sex or nationality. On its own plane it is relatively unencumbered but subjects itself to the limitations of incarnation in order to experience and express and as we have discussed, literally master form. We are not the form; we are the inner spiritual essence. It takes on what is known as the causal sheath which in turn takes on personalities in succession, until it has perfected its grasp of the use of matter and no longer needs this form of expression. We will get into exactly how that process occurs later on. For the moment I would like to keep it to that simple of an idea; an inner consciousness taking on a form and using it for a purpose.

In order to put this in easy terms I will incorporate an analogy created by my father that uses a computer operator. This operator is given a task of using a particular computer to handle the inventory of a manufacturing concern. The computer in question has the software and hardware he will need to assess the inventory, run reports and handle all of the other metrics involved in the management of the inventory for the company. Through the term of his tenure as the inventory man, he develops certain skills and efficiencies and even alters the way the inventory is processed with these new skills and techniques.

He has done a good job and soon the owner of the company decides he has a more important project for this operator. The company has grown and he needs someone to handle the payroll records. Our operator friend is now sitting in front of a brand new and more powerful computer but it is different, because there is a new purpose in mind. None of the software for the management of inventory is included and he is now using a different application. He has to learn and re-train on this new piece of equipment but what he brings with him are the skills he developed while using the other software. He is a better operator and will learn this new program and fulfill his purpose based on the growth he experienced in his last job.

In this analogy the Soul is obviously the operator and the three fold human personality is the computer. In each incarnation the computer is programmed by the experiences it has on the physical plane. We are on some level the accumulated reactions and responses (note those words) to our environmental circumstances. It is also pre-programmed by the Soul, with what it will need in this cycle. In our computer analogy that would be either the inventory or payroll software. The program exists as a mere tendency or potentiality until it is filled with information, and then put to use by the user, or the *consciousness*.

There are people with innate musical ability who never learn to play an instrument, as well as those with sharp minds who are never exposed to a deep educational process that could bring out genius. There may be no need to take those pre-programmed tendencies into the next cycle but the growth experienced brings a more effective operator to the next task, *because these potentials have been developed and expressed*. The Soul records growth in its journey. It does not accumulate experiences or memories. These are held in the mind and accessed by the physical brain as alluded to by Lao Tzu in the earlier part of this chapter.

This is kind of a gift in the system. Until a certain point is reached, referred to as the Transfiguration or Third Initiation, the Soul cannot bring with it into incarnation, the ability to access the history of events in its migration. Some people are able to access and read these events in the "Akashic Records" in a limited way, but that does not constitute the full *causal awareness* of the Soul while in incarnation. This aspect of the process eliminates the possibility of what could be painful information about past *lives* from effecting the current situations, goals, or karmic debt to be paid. It also could be seen as delaying or distracting if someone was aware of good past accomplishments and had an inflated sense of self as a result. For whatever reason, this information is not carried along, but the strengths and tendencies which do come through are a palpable explanation for child prodigies playing concert instruments, while their cultural siblings are playing with blocks.

Let's take a moment to talk about this growth process and how the Soul uses experience to further its evolutionary unfoldment, by returning to the concept of the automobile. A little over one hundred years ago we saw the beginning of its proliferation in the United States. The first models were capable of moving about five miles per hour and were powered by steam engines. They were extremely heavy requiring tracks to run on and really evolved into what we call railroad trains. The first real *cars* were the individual powered carts without horses. This of course involved a steering mechanism and a motor - technically a car, but not exactly useful. It was however, a new and unique experience for anyone who got to ride in one.

This limited but new experience leads us to come up with ideas that will make it a little better. Horses were still actually faster, so it's just a novelty until we address its speed. The bumpy ride leads to the development of a suspension system. The steering wheel is developed as a more comfortable way of keeping the vehicle under control than the original *stick*, using the leverage afforded by gearing etc. Through all of these developments, we are seeing the process of the creator coming up with innovations in successive models of vehicles, with the goal of a better driving experience.

The old models are not only improved as they are used, they lead to the development of better new models and the concept "automobile" as we explored earlier is developed and evolved, while at the same time the experience of the driver is evolved and not by any single consciousness as we understand it. It evolves by some unseen force of progress in the human consciousness as a whole, or in this case, the subset of those who were fortunate enough to have these particular experiences. This is representative of the evolutionary drive toward new and better experience in form and the expression of the new awareness garnered in the process, necessitating the next cycle of experience in a divine circular flow of creative energy.

This is a lower correspondence to the process undergone by the Soul as it moves from vehicle to vehicle gaining in experience and expressing the heightened awareness in the next cycle or incarnation. If I am purifying my body through my lifestyle, I will make a new one of similar refinement and be prone (through the level of consciousness achieved) to taking good care of that one too. If I have attained emotional control and mental acuity, it stands to reason that I will construct my new body with a similar level of refinement, if it fits my intended purpose to do so. I am constantly reconstructing this one; replacing it completely over and over during a single lifetime, so why in the greater cycle should we assume something different will occur? That is, unless it serves some specific Karmic obligation for me to incarnate in a body that is physically, mentally, or emotionally disabled.[37] This concept lays the responsibility at the feet of the individual, to create and recreate himself and his world.

There are other factors involved here too. We say you live in the universe you create but it's easy to argue against the principles involved here and say for instance: "Well, I didn't create the traffic jam that made me late, which caused the loss of an important account, and subsequently my job. I'm the victim of circumstance." Well, your decisions over time evidently added up to a situation that meant if you lost that account your job was in jeopardy, which really means your job was already in jeopardy. We cannot look at individual events in a sterile environment. Any understanding we gain would not apply in the

---

[37]   This is how I interpret Jesus' statement about the blind man. He was born blind "that the works of God should be made manifest in him." This can be a sacrifice made during the particular incarnation for the education of the Soul's companions on the lighted way.

real world. Everything interacts and we are looking for patterns of behavior that result in cultural systems and morays, or in the case of the individual, life patterns.

Let's say for arguments sake he missed his meeting because of a late flight delayed by a storm, rather than a traffic jam he might have avoided with the right planning. That could not be his fault, right? It is obvious that in this case he did not create what amounted to that last straw. He did create enough question and issue within his career that it was one more mistake and he was gone. If he had the right relations with the customer (and his boss) and his reputation was impeccable then the late flight would have become an amazing story of what he overcame, or perhaps didn't overcome, to be at that meeting. It could be a story that he used over and over in presentations and actually furthered his career. You are creating your life every day and you have been doing it forever. In my example other people were on that plane, and not all of them lost a job over the delay.

Decisions accrue in a kind of evolutionary telos. We hear about the polls on TV asking whether or not the country is "moving in the right direction." The country alluded to in this question is a conceptual aphorism for the group destiny of its people. It is not the piece of land it occupies, which is not moving in any practical sense. Although boundaries on the physical plane do fluctuate it is the group identity that matters. If the group in a new or conquered land is assimilated, it becomes part of the identity of the newly expanded group.

National, racial, family, religious, and other groupings think, feel and act collectively and will produce Karma collectively. On all of these levels, we see a sort of communal identity is created by the mere existence of the group. There are books about crowd mentality written for the purpose of understanding and reaching (or manipulating and agitating) a crowd because it will assume a common identity through shared experience very quickly. The things our governments do in our names carry consequences for us as individuals whether or not we travel abroad. We will reap what we sow. Families suffer the consequences of the actions of their members in the same way. You need only look around you at your own life, no matter where in the world you live, to see this playing out. The law does not change because of scale. It is universal. Every cause has an effect and every effect is the result of a cause.

There is more. If we are trying simply to create something just like everyone else is creating, like a decent job or a comfortable place to live, then we are moving along with the stream so to speak. We are all the creators of our own lives but we are co-creating with everyone else that's here too. Our individual dreams aggregate into the greater dream of the group, or nation. If we want to create something extraordinary in our lives we need a lot more personal power and we have to be much better at creating. We have to take conscious control of the process, or at least our little piece of it. We also must foster, as a group, an environment which has this freedom of expression in mind. This way we can live a diverse life as a community, maximizing the breadth of human expression and experience and so, conscious expansion.

Let's revisit the idea of the Soul in another way. It is said that the Soul on its own plane is perfect, but here, in what we ironically call the real world, we seldom see anything approaching perfection in our fellow man. If all I have said thus far is true, that sure seems like a contradiction but we can see a correlation to this in the perfection of an infant. We speak in terms of her whole life being ahead of her, and we know she is perfect. She is indeed perfect in her pure essence, though none of that seemingly unlimited potential has been expressed as yet.

We can think about it in terms of a magnetic tape, or in our days I guess a hard drive is more appropriate. It comes off the assembly line in perfect working order, yet nothing has been stored on it. It is blank and to an extent, useless, until it is exposed to the process of the recording of information.

Now it has to be remembered that the information is as useless without the mechanism as the mechanism is without the information. Consciousness needs form in the same way to express itself, so the analogy holds true to that point at least.

We can fill this memory device with beautiful sounds and images or we can fill it with hate and horror. The information can also affect the medium on which it is stored. The patterns have been emblazoned into the structure of the media and if they are destructive, as in a computer virus, they can slow or otherwise effect its operation and even damage it to the point where it must be discarded. In the next cycle a new mind and body are created by the Soul with all of the new potential. The experiences of beauty or horror contribute to the substance of the next form of expression as well as the circumstances chosen for its field of play, and a new purpose to be achieved.

Good and Evil?

This discussion could not be considered complete without at least a cursory look at the concept of good and evil. Karma is seen as good and bad because of our value judgments as a culture. The Cantonese symbol for crisis is the same as the symbol for opportunity. Obviously there is a slight divide between our culture in the West and that idea, from the East. The good news is there is no bad Karma. Instant Karma is not "gonna get ya." The bad news is there is no good Karma. It is not punitive, or favoritive. It is impersonal. If I drop a glass on the floor and it breaks, it does not make the floor (or me) evil. Now, the same act could be considered evil if I broke it intentionally to hurt someone's feelings. I will pay a price for that. Intent is huge.

Fire is not good or evil. Neither is electricity, gravity, atomic energy, or gun powder. It is the intent behind their use that raises the question. You create your life with your intent. You have exactly what you are entitled to and what you need. You cannot be given what you don't deserve or denied what you have earned. For all practical intents and purposes within the context of this work and the esoteric sciences in general, we are all united by the motivating force behind all creation. Recognition of this fact leads to an inclusive attitude. Anything that moves us toward a fuller expression of that recognized unity, and which is in harmony with the purpose of the expansion of consciousness, can be considered good. Any expression of selfish or separative intent, such as the gathering of power and resources for a confused concept of the illusory separate self, could be considered to be evil.

As we proceed it will be helpful to keep this idea in mind; the personality, whose composition we will discuss momentarily, is an input / output device for the Soul. As alluded to in our second key, we get to express our *selves* and experience each other, in a way that is only possible in the physical world. Remember, life is an infinite spectrum of rhythmic, cyclic, vibrations. We can find harmony in these infinite octaves of vibration, or live in a world of dissonance through our own failure to recognize the relationships between the chords of ourselves, our lives, and the universe we share.

CHAPTER 6

The Anatomy Of Consciousness

It is time we got into some depth about the true nature of the human being. We are going to go a lot deeper than just the physical frame, and endeavor to characterize in a useful way, the different facets of our overall composition. This will really paint a picture of the meaning behind our fifth and sixth keys in that we are a multi-layered consciousness. It also incorporates the principles in keys two and four. I hope you are beginning to see how deeply inter-related all of these principles are. The universe is one life, expressing and experiencing a world as it self-creates in cycle, after cycle, within cycle, embracing all of the fundamental precursors within the newly emergent levels of expression, in a complex and remarkably elegant dance.

As we will now see, humanity in all its uniqueness serves as a beautiful diagram of the entire process. Even science acknowledges that we all have a mind, an emotional nature, as well as the physical body but I am sure we will part company pretty quickly on their qualities and function. Most religions and some philosophers acknowledge the presence of an indwelling thinker or Soul. The Ageless Wisdom carries these ideas much deeper than many of the disciplines we have mentioned and as open minded investigators, we don't want to leave out any possibilities that might make sense.

The first idea that I would like to posit is that even if you are completely unfamiliar with the concepts we are about to address, most of you know at least some of this information intuitively. Some of it may ring a bell immediately and other ideas may seem outrageous in the beginning and start to make more sense as we continue.

What does it mean to be human? Can we limit our definition to a two armed, two legged, intelligent creature that walks upright? Perhaps on the surface this would seem adequate but what if you only had one leg? How human would you be? What about emotions? Some think that is what divides us from the Animal Kingdom but animals exhibit emotion. Elephants mourn their dead. We have all heard a mother dog cry when her puppies are taken away. Incidentally, cattle cry for weeks when their calves are taken. These are creatures with feelings, even if you can only see them as food.

What about the mind? You can have a horribly disfigured body and a fully functional mind. One of the outstanding theoretical physicists of our time, Steven Hawking, lived most of his life in a body that could not survive on its own. As his physical health deteriorated he was kept going by the universal health care system in Britain, which is maligned in the US as Socialism. He communicated with words formed by computer circuits and sent through a speaker, because he was no longer capable of using his body to do it.

All of these aspects combine within the human being, and yet none of them *are* the human being. It could be said that it is the dweller within, or the individualized Soul or consciousness which is in fact what *is* human. I will posit now that this too is an expression of something greater; the true individualized spark of the cosmic flame, the Monad. Up to this point we have treated Soul and Monad as a single idea but perhaps it is time we made the distinction. Man is a trinity of Spirit, Soul, and body. The Monad is an indivisible fragment of the One Life or consciousness. It uses the Soul in the same way the Soul uses the personality, as a medium of expression.

71

Again, for simplicity's sake we will start with the body that we all know, and work our way up to the more refined and rarified nature expressing through it. For the purpose of this conversation I will ask that you consider that above all else, you are a unit of consciousness. Then it is of no concern whether you are male or female, or if your skin is brown or pale, or for that matter, the number of legs or arms you possess. Each of us is a human consciousness and at the same time a part of many forms of aggregate or group consciousness. As we discussed in the chapter on Reincarnation and Karma our family has an identity, as does our race, nationality, religion, and most importantly, humanity itself.

The human personality is a threefold expression of the indwelling Soul. This is used as a probe is used by a scientist; to explore and experience an environment in which he cannot function with his physical body, like the bottom of the ocean. In the case of the Soul it has no physical body, so it creates one in order to explore the physical world, but that's not enough. There are Seven Planes of Manifestation in our solar system. The human personality is designed to function on the lower three; the Physical, Emotional and Mental Planes.

These seven planes are all like phases or harmonic levels of vibration. If you tried to visualize them as a layer cake with the most dense at the bottom, they would progressively be the Physical, Astral, Mental, Buddhic, Atmic, Monadic, and the finest called Adi. The physical plane as well as all of the others can be divided into seven sub planes, and in the instance of the physical there are the dense, liquid, gaseous, and four ethers.

In order to really "live" we need more than just a physical mechanism or "soft machine."[38] In addition to action, we must be capable of sentience or feeling and a higher expression of that, known as emotion. There is a sentient response mechanism that works with the soft machine called the Astral Body. Now, we can all imagine what it would be like if we were capable of feeling and acting but not thinking. The world today is

---

[38] William S. Burroughs – *The Soft Machine* (New York: Grove Press, 1961)

a reflection of the fact that most of us are really living in an emotional consciousness or focus.

In order to interpret and process the information coming in there is a mental or Manasic Body as well. Manas is the principle of mind, and gives man his name. When we say "human" we are speaking of "the one who thinks." Interestingly, this is the translation of "homo sapien" as well. These three bodies are used to explore the lower three worlds or planes of manifestation (physical, emotional and mental). They are interactive because the outer planes are made up of the substance of the inner, but for another perspective they can be thought of as dimensions. The act of fighting for an idea or ideal is actually very odd. You cannot attack or defend a thought or feeling physically. Beating someone up cannot really change what they think on a given subject, perhaps just what they think of you. They only submit physically because that is the dimension on which they are being attacked. These three bodies are sometimes referred to as the lower quaternary because of the dual nature of the physical and this is where we begin.

The Physio-Etheric Body

First, we will address the physical body. This, for all practical purposes, can be considered an automaton. It is quite literally a soft machine. It reacts to the world but is not the cause of anything with regard to health and well-being. A powerful, effective and durable physical body is the result of good health, not the cause of it. All ailment except injury (and that's arguable too) is caused in one of the other energetic counterparts we are about to discuss.

Einstein tells us that all is energy. When we look at something solid, it is actually made of constantly moving atomic and sub-atomic particles and as we discussed, lots of empty space. This is the vital energy that underpins or sub-stands physical reality. This is the true substance of things. It is the electrical charge we feel in our nervous system and the nervous system is its outward manifestation. The Etheric body is like a web of free flowing energy but it also forms channels which are called meridians. These meridians intersect and combine at various points in the body and form centers or Chakras (wheels). In areas where many intersect (twenty-one) we have a major center. These meridians and centers are the basis for the ancient practice of acupuncture. The acupuncturist uses needles inserted in very specific locations in an attempt to rebalance the flow of this energy.

The Etheric Body forms a cell by cell replica of the physical structure in a sense but it is really the physical structure that is the replica because the energy is the source. A dead cell does not divide. It is the life that creates the body not vice versa. It sounds incredible but if you think about it, every cell is alive and electric. Those lives interact and their proximity to each other is the result of the cohesion of this field of intelligent organizing force. Stomach cells will always get replaced by stomach cells but all types of cells were originally created from stem cells in the embryo. This is why they are seen with such anticipation in their possible medical uses. The body is an intricate design built and constantly re-built according to a plan. Science is beginning to understand some of the codes and can trigger stem cells to create specific desired cell types.

The etheric energy also radiates and extends beyond the physical structure by about an inch. This is dependent on the level of vitality in the body. In fact the etheric double is sometimes referred to as the *vital body*. It has been photographed by Kirlian photography[39] since the 1940's and can be shown to change as the person drinks alcohol or changes his activities. I have personally experimented with this and seen changes in the photographs taken when I was doing math or thinking of someone I loved as an image was exposed.

---

[39]   Kirlian photography is photographic technique used to capture electrical coronal discharges. It uses a high voltage coil to create a charge around a photographic plate, or in my experience, a Polaroid cartridge, upon which objects or fingers are placed producing an image on the film without exposure to visible light.

Prana and Vitality

The Etheric body or *doppelganger* is fed by what are called Pranic fluids. We get Prana from the air we breathe and the food we eat, as well as from sunlight. There are four different grades of this Etheric energy or Prana and our health and vitality depends upon how much and of which type we are assimilating. Meat has the highest concentration of the lowest or coarsest form of Prana. It is very dense and of very little use to the body. Physically it takes more energy to digest. This leads to that heavy full feeling that meat eaters will miss if they consume a salad alone for a meal. This *sticks to the ribs* feeling is not a healthy one. The idea that eating muscle tissue will make it easier for the body to make muscle tissue is ridiculous. All protein has to be broken down into its component parts (amino acids) before the body can do anything with them. Horses have plenty of muscle and they don't eat meat or drink cow's milk. Food is not only our fuel but the building blocks used in constructing and constantly reconstructing the body as well. If you change what you eat now, your body will begin to construct itself of those better materials and grow healthier over time. It is never too late to alter an ongoing process.

If we are eating in a healthy manor and using our bodies every day we are:

1. Less likely to get sick.
2. Recover more quickly if we do get ill.
3. Heal more quickly if we are injured.
4. In the case of a child, grow faster and stronger.

In every case it is a matter of the level of vitality in the body that makes the difference. We all intuitively know this. This you may not know. About 25% of our illnesses originate in the Etheric Body, as the result of an imbalance or blockage of the flow of this vital energy. Whether we are considering the vascular, glandular, respiratory, or energetic systems of the body, stagnation is not a good thing.

Vegetables or plant matter exhibit a higher concentration of the finer forms of Prana. As we know vegetation converts the suns energy into its own physical form and vitality. When we consume raw plant matter it is still living and has most of its Prana intact but cooked or not, it is easier for our bodies to process. This is one of the reasons for a vegetarian diet. We can talk about diet further once we have established a few more ideas.

We also get much of our Prana and vitality from our breath. The problem is that in the West, we don't know how to breathe. That may sound silly but did anyone ever teach you? We tend to breathe in a very shallow manner in the top of our lungs, never really breathing deeply unless we exert ourselves during some form of activity. We need to learn to breathe deep into our bellies (like a singer) all day long. This will bring that vital energy deep into our etheric bodies and help us fight disease and generally feel better. This is part of many forms of Yoga and the breath is often controlled during many forms of meditation. Of course all practice of Yoga is discipline, no matter what specific school you may find as your path to union. It is not a good idea to try to use deep breathing exercises without guidance or without incorporating other aspects of these disciplines. This is because you can overdose on Prana. In my first two years of meditation training in the Arcane School the only breathing exercise was the correct use of the OM. Just like too much sun, the vitalizing force of the breath is not to be toyed with.

The best we can do is start by eating finer LIVE foods, play in the sun and breathe deeply. When your food is alive you are eating LIFE. See how it makes you feel. It is one of the easiest aspects of the path. Purification of the physical body and returning it to optimum health makes all of the other steps on the path possible.

Now let's look at how an imbalance in this energetic system can manifest as dis-ease. As any doctor would, we will start with an assessment of the symptoms. For argument's sake we will assume I am having a pain in my neck. The muscles are tight and I am stiff and in pain. What is actually happening on an energetic level is that congestion on one or more of the meridians is causing a point of tension, the muscle is contracting and it cannot *let go*. This is causing me discomfort and disrupting the normal flow of bodily fluids in the area because of the contraction of the muscle. This prompts me to go to a healer like an acupuncturist and he stimulates specific points along the meridians to get that energy flowing again. In some cases an electrical current is induced through the needles to help this to begin. Energy in the etheric body must continue flowing as the blood in your circulatory system must constantly flow to do its job. If blood pools, ill health ensues. Sedentary lifestyles do not lead to good health. Life is motion on all levels.

Magnetic or light healers can help to balance me out again as well. Massage can temporarily relieve the resultant tension. The problem is that if I don't change whatever was causing the symptoms, they will return. This particular issue is not likely to have been caused in the etheric body, which is why I chose it. The example I picked would more likely be caused in my Astral or emotional body and could be a mental issue, if that is what is stressing me out. An energy healer may not be appropriate in this case because they remove the warning signals that had the effect of slowing me down. When the pain is gone the pace continues and something worse may come about. I could end up with an ulcer or cancer. The entire person must be treated in every case or a disservice may be rendered with the best of intentions.

The Chakras

As I mentioned earlier, this web of energy that makes up the Etheric body runs along meridians which have been traced along the body. Where there are many intersecting channels of energy a center or Chakra exists. There are seven major centers within the human body and we are going to deal with them, and a few of the intermediary ones as well. The seven major centers form a straight line up the spine. In the case of each of the centers we see a physical manifestation as a gland or other organ in the body.

At the base of the spine we find the first center or *root chakra*. The physical manifestation of this center is seen in the spinal cord itself. Moving up the spine we have the sacral center in the area of the genitals and they are the physical manifestation of this very creative energy center. Moving higher in the area of the solar plexus we have the next, called the solar plexus center. In the chest area is the coronal or heart center represented by the thymus gland. It is important to remember that these centers are not actually at the locations of the organs that represent them physically. They are in the area of the spine and originate behind the spine.

The throat or laryngeal center has its physical manifestation in the thyroid glands, and then there are two major centers in the head. They are the ajna center (pronounced anya) behind the brow and the crown center at the top of the head. The ajna center is sometimes thought of as the third eye but that is a misconception caused by its location. Its physical counterpart is the pituitary gland and the one for the crown center is the pineal gland.

When the centers in the head are awakened and active, interaction between the two major centers and a minor center at the base of the skull called the alta major center (represented physically by the carotid gland) begins. Triangles of energy are formed by the right and left eye along with each of these energy centers as they increase in activity and this causes the third eye to open. This will happen naturally as a result of the treading of the path and need not be concentrated upon. We will note that as we go along. There is no need to force anything, as these centers will awaken due to the activities of study, meditation and service.

Kundalini and the Lower Triangle

There are some interesting interactions and associations between these centers which are worth mentioning, even in a cursory study such as this. The two lowest centers (root and sacral) are concerned with the development of the physical being. The next three centers (solar plexus, heart, and throat) are concerned with the development of the personality and character of the individual, and the head centers with the spiritual development. The average human being is operating from the bottom five with the heart and throat centers just becoming active. The aspirant and disciple are awakening the top two.

The three lower centers are the seat of activity in the average human being and are all located below the diaphragm, which effectively divides the torso in two. They form what is referred to as the lower triangle and they are aligned with the activities related to the survival of the entity. Instincts such as the search for food and shelter as well as reproduction are governed here. The lower triangle represents Will (solar plexus), Love (sacral), and Intelligent Activity (root), in a lower or personality based expression.

Within the root center dwells a fiery force referred to as Kundalini or the *Serpent Fire*. This energy forms seven concentric spheres of force, and when the human being is on the path of probation and initiation it begins to stir. In the average person this force is barely trickling but as the aspirant or disciple progresses, it will rise up the spinal column with increasing power, and it does so in an interesting triple manner.

The first stream of energy is known as Ida and it is considered negative in polarity. It rises up in a serpentine manner (hence the name) through the centers from the bottom to the top. The next, called Pingala, is considered positive in polarity and rises up in a similar, though opposite manner to the first, intersecting it at every one of the centers and giving the appearance of stacked 8's. The third is known as Shushumna and is considered neutral as far as polarity is concerned. It rises straight up the spine. The description above will paint a picture of a symbol which had been used by the American Medical Association for decades, despite its ancient associations with Alchemy. It is called the Caduceus and has two serpents wrapped around a staff with a ball of light and wings at the top. To complete the symbol it is necessary to add the wings of Mercury, symbolizing the consciousness which takes flight once these forces are flowing. As the fire rises up the spine it burns away the *etheric web* that is essentially a series of barriers between the centers protecting against premature flow. Interestingly, if you look at the symbol in use by the AMA now, in their modernization they have removed one of the serpents and literally leaned it to one side. This is a more appropriate representation of the staff of Asclepius and simultaneously represents a deep irony. It is amazing that these highly trained and educated people would use a symbol so out of balance without even realizing how appropriate it is to the one-sided practice of allopathic medicine.

The Upper Triangle

The upper centers are sometimes referred to as the upper triangle, even though there are actually two centers in the head. These are barely active in the average human being and are becoming active in the probationer on the path. It is the task at hand for the disciple to higher consciousness to bring the focus of the life into higher expression. This means higher mental activity, higher emotional activity and even higher physical activity in the form of service. One of the tasks of the spiritual traveler is to transmute the personality expressions of the lower triangle and focus those energies through the upper centers.

The Solar Plexus center is the seat of instinctive activity and the clearing house for all of the lower emotional responses. That is why we feel like we have been hit in the stomach when we witness something negative or are told some news that is disturbing to us. We need to move that activity into the heart center. The creative activity that emanates from the sacral center needs to be migrated into the throat center and expressed as a higher form of creativity, rather than physical pro-creation. The animal cunning that keeps the body safe and is shared with the Animal Kingdom must be migrated into the head, and acted upon appropriately through use of the intellect and the intuition. Through this shift we become identified with the higher source rather than the lower reflection. It is a matter of identification and focus on what are existing, yet relatively dormant aspects of our selves.

The crown center is the most important for the purposes of spiritual awakening. When this center is highly active it often results in the light in the head that is described by those who have become *Enlightened*.

There are said to be a thousand cells surrounding the pineal gland which light up in activity. It is called the Solomon center and in the legend, Solomon's one thousand wives are symbolic representations of these cells. This is the light that blinded Saul of Tarsus for three days on the road to Damascus, producing from him, St. Paul. I believe the burning bush Moses described was a subjective light, not outside his body. He had glimpsed the "all-consuming fire" in his consciousness. The limitations of language, and the low level of sophistication in the populace left him little choice in his description. How would you describe such a localized light to people who had never seen light from a source other than fire, lightning or the sun? The timeless nature of the truth related to us in scripture leads us to forget that it was written at a time when human consciousness was far less evolved and life was very simple. The fact that there are people who claim they know which bush it was and lead tourists to it today speaks of the inability to understand the symbolism used to transmit spiritual teaching.

The Astral Body

Before we get into our description of the Astral Body, let's clear up a few misconceptions. The word astral simply means starry and this type of energy is actually more appropriately characterized by mist and miasma. The word was used in Theosophical writings, and it stuck. Eckhart Tolle calls this the pain body, and that is a much more accurate description I'm sorry to say. We hear about things like astral travel and many of us may not know what to associate with that. It's not space flight. The Astral Plane, on which the Astral Body functions, is the plane of emotions. This is also known as the cosmic liquid plane, so when we are talking about anything emotional we use liquid metaphors, like storms or waves of emotion. I have felt a literal wave of feeling overcome my body.

The Astral Body is your response mechanism to the emotional plane and is made up of the matter of that plane. The Akashic Records are actually the emotional records of the universe. Akasha is astral and so, some of what is taken from those records and believed whole heartedly by the reader could be glamour or illusion.[40] Perhaps this is something desired strongly, that has never come to pass. We must always be alert and aware and make no assumptions about the information to which we are exposed. Another thing we can note is the fact that much of what can be said about the Astral Body can also be said of the Manasic Body, on a higher plane of expression.

So, interpenetrating the dense physical body and its etheric counterpart is another, made up of the energy on another plane of existence. It extends beyond the limits of the physical body much farther than the etheric, and it vibrates within a different frequency range. Not all of the particles are the same. Each has its own frequency signature and affinities based on prior interactions. Again, we use the metaphor of lower vibrations in connection with the lower emotional responses like hate and fear, and higher representing the higher selfless emotions leading up to universal love, which is really not emotion at all.

Anything you feel, whether an emotion or even the sensation from touching something, is transmitted to your consciousness by your Astral Body. 50% of our illnesses originate there. They must *precipitate* down through the etheric as in our example before. If I am tied up in emotional knots, my body will be tied up in physical knots as well. Now, this is very closely associated with mind. Desire can and does color our thoughts. We all know that you can worry yourself sick. Well, you can think yourself sick too.

The Sanskrit word for the principle involved is Kama. The principle of the mental plane is called Manas and this close interaction leads to the term Kama/Manas or desire/mind. It's very rare to have a thought without feeling or a feeling devoid of thought but it does happen, as in the case of unthinking anger.

---

40   Glamour is defined in the Ageless Wisdom as an emotional form of Illusion; the word illusion referring to a mental aspect of the same type of false image or impression.

I'm not sure of the technical process involved, but the aura can now be photographed. They are not photographing the astral matter itself because the hand is laid onto a set of sensors, and the energy detected is then superimposed over the person's photograph. They do bear out the emotional state of the person and are interpreted that way. Reflexology is a system of mapping and working with etheric energies and shows a representation of the entire body, on the combined surfaces of the hands (or feet). The emotional state precipitates downward through the etheric and is evidently being sensed on that plane through the electrical sensors. While the astral matter is not sensed directly, its effects are seen. Science contends with this problem constantly in the form of mathematical imbalances caused by particles we cannot yet detect. This is how a science as empirical as physics can evolve into something theoretical.

The Manasic Body

In much the same way, interpenetrating all we have been considering, is yet another energetic vehicle comprised of a more rarified material. This is the mental or Manasic Body and consists again of both the substance and surrounding mental energy. The physical body has an aggregate mind that holds it together, heals it and makes it grow and function. This is the source of so-called *muscle memory*. Again, every cell in my body has mind in a lower level of expression and in their aggregate is formed the mind of the physical body.

The individual human mind is a multi-layered condition, with what is called the lower or concrete mind, a Soul expression on a higher level known as the Son of Mind, and also a higher creative or abstract mind. These actually represent the Trinity of Intelligent Activity, Love, and *the Will to good* on the mental plane. The object of occult meditation is to develop the connection between the lower two and through this union gain access to the third. About 25% of our illness comes from the mental body, and again the imbalanced condition precipitates down through the astral and the etheric into the physical body and makes us sick.

The field of mental energy extends out even further from the physical than does the astral, and that is part of why masterminding and collaboration work so well. Thoughts can literally fly around a room, which in many cases is full of people who have worked closely together for some time - like writers who literally feed off of each other's thoughts. Just like the Astral Body that is sensitive to the mood of another person, the Manasic Body is sensitive to their thoughts.

Ella Wheeler Wilcox said "thoughts are things endowed with form and wings." To explore that world we need a vehicle that functions on that plane. Something sensitive to, and when sufficiently developed, able to interpret what Patanjali called the "raincloud of knowable things."[41] It is through the development and control of the lower mind that we reach the higher mind and then the intuition. Now you may be thinking "how does this all work; and when am I going to have one of those moments when this makes sense?"

Here I am, this physical body supercharged with energy and surrounded by it. I have a thought. Some idea crosses my mind. A pretty girl for instance. Now that thought can easily lead to desire and that is why I picked it. If the desire is sufficient, I may have a physical reaction as well. If this or any other idea fits some specific situation in my life right now, I may perk up a bit. My heart rate increases etc. This type of response can be evoked by the site of an object, such as a car, as well. We are talking about an emotional response to a thought. I want the result. The question becomes, how much do I want it?

Just having a thought never really got anything done. If I want action, I need the physical body to move. The problem is it only seems to move when it (or something as yet undefined) <u>wants</u> to move. In other words, desire is involved, so I have to go through the Astral Body to get anything done. If the desire is there I may act and a widget is born. Something is either created or altered. Luckily, as I said before, these

---

[41] This term comes from the Yoga Sutras of Patanjali, available with interpretation in the book by Alice A. Bailey - *The Light of the Soul* " (New York: Lucis Publishing Company, 1927)

two are very related. It is hard to have a thought without triggering an emotion and vice-versa. The problem is that every tool we have seems to have a trap on its other side. If we are focused on our desires themselves, we are not cultivating new ideas. If we are trapped in our minds or *our own little world*, nothing gets done. Balance is always the key.

Resonance

Now remember, all of this is energy and in accordance with our third key it's all vibrating and at varying rates. Sometimes harmony is the result and sometimes it is dissonance. This is the basis for some of the things we all know and recognize. One person in the household or a workplace who is sufficiently upset or angry, can easily overpower the mood of the entire environment. There's a TV commercial where this bad mood just goes running through an office. One woman gets yelled at and she smacks the coffee out of another guy's hand, then he shreds some other guy's work, etc. We all know this stuff goes on. Now we are looking at one explanation of how that is possible. What I think about and desire I will see manifest in my world. This is part of "The Secret."[42] It's not the Law of Attraction, it's the Law of Attraction *and Repulsion,* and it is based on resonance. I am constantly attracting and repelling astral, etheric, and mental matter (energy) all day and night. It would be worth your time to examine what you are dwelling on and resonating with in your subconscious. Look around you and you see the results. What are you experiencing? It is, in every case, what you are creating.

This is important, and it is one of the fundamental changes we have the power to make in our lives at any instant. Let's say I decide I am going to put myself in a loving state, and for argument's sake, we will assume I succeed. What is happening? I am consciously vibrating in what could euphemistically be called the key of love. Some of the astral matter around my body has that affinity, and begins to resonate in response. It's like the classroom experiment with tuning forks; you hit the "A" fork

---

[42]   Rhonda Byrne – *The Secret* (New York: Atria Books, 2006)

and all the other A's in the room ring. Think about how full the sound of a piano is. When you strike a key the hammer hits three strings tuned to different octaves of the same note. There are eight octaves on a full sized piano, so there are seven other sets of strings tuned to different "A's," all vibrating in resonance, if the strings are all tuned properly. In our case we are dealing with a sort of free flowing cloud of vibrating particles. Some of them are not resonant with this vibratory rhythm and what happens is that they get thrown off, only to be replaced by something that is. *I am attracting loving energy by feeling and resonating love.* What do you think will happen next time I decide to put myself in a loving state? It's easier! Provided I didn't wait too long. I am now more resonant with love and can continue to tune myself to it over time. It makes me more capable of love and less capable of hate and I'll add, less vulnerable to it.

What if I decide just to be passive? Is that OK? For example in meditation or just in my normal daily activities, I may decide to be passive and receptive. Well that makes you open to whatever may be coming by, so in your sanctum in meditation this can be of great help but in our daily interactions there is another factor to be considered. Let's look back at that one person at work. If I am just passive, her mood can have a bigger effect on me and much more quickly. Whether it is good or bad, (and nothing truly has intrinsic value) she is radiating something and I am placid. It's like dropping a pebble in a lake. If the waters are still, the effects will be felt across the entire lake and reflected back again. If on the other hand I am radiating love, I am making my own ripples glowing with harmonious loving energy. It may not be enough to change her mood, but it could stop her from being able to change mine. Jesus told us to love our enemies. It's not a platitude. If I love even those who hate me, I make myself immune to their hate. Anyone can hate back and resonate with that energy. Do not the publicans do the same? (Matt 5:46) To live in a loving state in the presence of hate is a true achievement.

I have tried this with success and offer up an experiment consciously engaged in by my second wife and me. I am a life-long musician, and we would frequent certain venues to see live music. One evening we decided before going out that we would try to consciously radiate love throughout the evening. We literally "lit ourselves up" in the car on the way. She went in ahead of me as I parked the car, and then I approached alone. A woman came out as I was walking in and grabbed me and hugged me. She was fairly tipsy, and that can make you react more easily to a feeling. I don't think it makes you more sensitive, just less inhibited. She told me that out of all of the people in the club she got a different kind of feeling from me and some woman she had run into inside. We walked back in and I introduced her to my wife but of course they had already met. In this crowded club and out front, this woman sensed something different about Louise and I. Something we had consciously decided to radiate.

Here is another somewhat more subtle example. I went on a solo walk into the wilderness outside of Crestone Colorado to stay overnight. I decided to try the same thing. The reason that the animals were not afraid of Jesus or Noah was because they were totally harmless in their nature. I decided to radiate love and harmlessness on my walk and see if I would come across more wildlife. I didn't really see anything unusual on my hike but as I was sitting in my campsite a big buck waltzed right in, sniffing at my pots. I have a photo of him with his nose inside of a soup can. This was a large buck and they are not often seen up close. The next morning I had sheep in my campsite. A whole family including the cutest baby you have ever seen. I had hiked five miles into this remote area and these are not trained animals looking for garbage cans. Although I was told I would probably see sheep up there I had no idea I would be dining with them.

Tuning Your Consciousness

Personally I find all of this fascinating but unless can we use it to make our lives better, what is the point? If we become observant of our state, we can begin to tune our consciousness to seize on other things. What does that mean? I bought a motorcycle a few years ago and suddenly I started noticing all of the motorcycles on the road.

They were everywhere. I had another bike many years ago and the same thing happened. I *got into it* and started recognizing the other bikes. Did the proportion of motorcycles to cars on the road change in the interim? Not in any significant way. I just started noticing them. Then something else overtook it in my consciousness and years went by without me paying any real attention to them. Only when it once again, came to the forefront in my thoughts (because I had bought another one) did I start noticing all of those bikes again. We are constantly re-tuning our consciousness. We just need to do it CONSCIOUSLY.

How? Think lofty thoughts! Read philosophy or quantum physics, or the Bible or Talmud. This will help purify and make harmless your thought process. In the same way that being loving helps you be more loving, thinking about things like charity and other types of virtuous ideals makes you more resonant with those types of thoughts. If you read Socrates and study him, you will begin to think like him and come up with thoughts and ideas that he may have created under similar circumstances. We see this concept in detective stories where once a detective begins to think like his prey, he is finally able to anticipate his next move and catch him.

This is where right aspiration and right speech come in. If I hate fat people, or Jews, or Muslims, Republicans or Democrats, whose mind am I poisoning? If I am running around cursing every driver on the road who makes a mistake or in my opinion is going too slow, I'm not affecting them, I'm affecting me. Even if I do set someone else off by flipping them the proverbial bird, I have succeeded in negatively affecting two people's days. Wow… I guess congratulations are in order. Taking it as a personal attack when someone cuts you off on the highway is a huge leap. Why and how would he have picked you? Why would he want to ruin your day? How important are you in the life of someone who simply happens to be travelling in the same direction at the same time you are? The truth is that you are so unimportant (to him) that he didn't even notice you. Perhaps that is the real gripe.

Wouldn't it be better to be the agent of a different kind of change? Casey Stengel was a revered baseball manager for the early NY Yankees. He was actually hated as a player and used to get booed every time he came to the plate, even at Yankee Stadium. One time he came out to bat and amidst the boo's, he bowed and tipped his hat, letting loose a sparrow he had tucked under it and they began to cheer. He flipped them a different kind of bird and they never booed him again.

One of the ancient symbols for humanity is the Lotus. This flower has its roots in the mud, the earth, a symbol of the physical plane. It has to grow up through the waters of the emotional plane to flower in the air of the mental plane. We need to purify it from the ground up. The mind is both the prison and the liberator, because we can just as easily get caught up inside our mind as our emotions. When you are thinking, you are not aware. You are not in what Eckhart Tolle calls "presence." Make sure that YOU are using YOUR mind and it is not using you.

The story of Narcissus is an allegory for the story of the Soul, our next subject. Narcissus is a mythical creature of exceptional beauty, who upon seeing his own reflection in a pool of water, became transfixed. He was in such awe of the beauty of his reflection that he could not bear to look away. There are two versions of this story and in one of them, he dies there of starvation. In the other more telling version, he falls into the water and drowns. The identification became with the reflected self, the product of consciousness and not consciousness itself. Did you get the symbolism of the water? It is the desire for the material world that holds us transfixed. That desire has to be transmuted into Spiritual Will, through aspiration.

With regard to the Astral Body, we need to raise its vibrations as well by practicing harmlessness and detachment. Now this sounds nice but again, how is it of use? When we are upset by something the Astral Body is in a literal state of siege. It is a violent storm surrounding the body and it is going to trigger anything in our surroundings that might be resonant. If you live with a partner or spouse, your bodies will be tuned very closely to each other. Unless one (or both) of you is capable of living in a perfect loving state at all times, you can trigger each other into a quickly escalating fight over nothing. We try to calm those waters through correct use of the mind, because we know now that it triggers emotion. We must detach ourselves from the outcome of the events in our lives, consistently taking the attitude of the observer.

On my 47th birthday I lost a job I had for over seven years. My brother called that morning, not to say happy birthday, but to tell me a law suit in which we were involved was all but dead. My wife and I had just finished a conversation surrounding the end of child support coming in for my then college aged stepson. I looked at my wife and said "it will be interesting to see how all of this works out," as if I was watching a movie of someone else's life. I could have gone into a depression or started drinking again and many people would have said something like, "well what do you expect?" Instead, I just observed and had a pretty good day. I spent some time looking for work and as I write this years later, I acknowledge that I lived through some turmoil but I'm still OK.

With regard to the Physio-Etheric body, we need to keep it vitalized through proper exposure to sunlight, proper breathing and proper eating. So let's talk about that for a moment before we bring in the Soul.

Vegetarianism

There are some who would insist that a vegetarian diet is necessary for spiritual awakening. This is both true and not true. A vegetarian diet will not make you spiritual. If you are following the path and disciplining and awakening yourself, there will probably come a time when you will lose your desire to eat meat. It will be a symptom of your awakening, not a trigger to it. The good news is you don't have to run from the spiritual path because you are attached to eating meat.

There are a few really important reasons for a vegetarian diet in addition to simply being against killing animals. There is nothing wrong with doing it for that reason alone and you will still benefit from it. As meat eaters are prone to argue, we kill plants to eat them too, although most of the time we simply take the fruit or seed pod of whatever sort, and the plant survives. The physical effect of this change will be the lightening or enlivening of the etheric body with the finer Prana in the food. This is an act of purification that will help you to handle the energies you will begin to encounter through disciplines like meditation. A narrow gauge wire snaps under the same current that will pass easily through a wire of a greater gauge or capacity. The level of the purity of the copper in the wire has the same impact.

The second thing it does is to take another step in moving away from our own animal nature. When we eat animal flesh we are re-enforcing that which we wish to diminish. Man is said to be a God (consciousness) riding on a beast. Mary was riding an ass while pregnant with Jesus. The centaur is another symbol for mankind that holds this idea. Man is where highest consciousness or *Spirit* and the lower *form* meet. Just as the energy in your aura is affected by a passerby or a loved one, the energy within your aura is obviously affected by you (the consciousness). The cells in your body, though they are unaware of the needs or functioning of the whole, are affected by it as well. We, as conscious units, are a part of the consciousness we call God/Life and we are just as unaware of the intentions of that whole as our blood cells are of our conscious intent.

One of the byproducts of human evolution is that of redemption. We literally uplift the frequency of the matter in our bodies by its proximity to our consciousness. The Gospel of Thomas says "blessed is the lion who is eaten by a man because the lion becomes the man. Cursed is the man that is eaten by the lion because the man becomes the lion." This is illustrative to a degree, but that which truly defines the man (his consciousness) endowed the body with its attributes. Only the form was devoured by the lion, the "man" escaped.

Not only is the matter you are consuming endowed with certain qualities because it was part of an animal, but this is in many cases, an unhealthy and unhappy animal. It is also an animal that is in a state of extreme panic and fear when it is killed. As we have discussed, we can think ourselves sick with anxiety. When you eat an animal killed in this way you are also eating the animals fear. It is a product of all of these negative emotions and will affect you in very negative ways.

CHAPTER 7

The Soul

The principle of Soul is the principle of consciousness and the Soul itself is the consciousness aspect of the human being. The Soul is connected to the personality with a triple bridge of light reaching the outer planes from the inner. The two that are commonly referenced are (1) the life thread or Sutratma, and (2) the consciousness thread, called the Antahkarana, or *rainbow bridge*. The Antahkarana is known as both the entire bridge and also as the consciousness portion. It is like the Will aspect of the Trinity in that it is known as a part and the whole simultaneously. Later, the third comes into play and that has to do with creativity. This rainbow bridge is like a thread of light and when it is developed sufficiently during incarnation, the communication from the Soul is what drives the human being forward and the purposes of the current cycle are more effectively accomplished.

The Soul resides in a stasis of sorts within what is known as the Causal Body in between incarnations, bearing out the lessons of the last cycle and then preparing for the next. When it is ready, it will once again enter the lower three worlds, or planes of manifestation. The Antahkarana carries the qualities of our consciousness from one incarnation to the next in a very interesting manner, and serves as the mode of energetic exchange and communication between the various aspects of spirit, mind, and body. I will caution you, that this will not likely be one of those moments of bell ringing clarity… How does this indwelling thinker acquire and then use a body and why would this magnificent free expression of consciousness make such a sacrifice?

Well, the "why" we kind of covered in the beginning. In order to experience the physical world (Key Two) one must become a part of that physical world (as well as the other two) so it sends out its probe, into these environments where it cannot function itself. Upon this thread of energy projected on to the lower planes are strung what are called the "permanent atoms." There is a physical, an astral, and a mental permanent atom. Now don't get stuck on the word atom. The cartoon you saw as a kid was just that, a cartoon. The word atom was adopted to represent the atom of science. Its original meaning was an indivisible unit. In a sense the cell is an atom of the body, and man's consciousness an atom of the whole of consciousness.

The mental permanent atom carries with it all of the qualities of your thought patterns and capacity for thought. Not the thoughts themselves but the effects of having experienced thought. As we discussed earlier, you are to a great degree the result of all of the thoughts, ideas and experiences of your lifetime. You don't remember all of it but you are still the product of those thoughts. Many of our tendencies come from our formative years, and are a result of the nature of our family of origin. The physical permanent atom contains all of the information necessary to form the physical being needed and in a sense deserved in the next incarnation. Similarly, the emotional permanent atom contains impressions of all of the characteristics of the emotional being to be brought to life.

The Soul uses these permanent atoms to convey the characteristics, not the experiences themselves. It is how the Soul carries the benefits from one life to the next. If you had to start over without the effects of earlier cycles, then the cyclic process would have no purpose. If you believe a Soul has only one cycle of birth and death, then it still needs a way to determine what characteristics the body, mind and emotions will have. We are all the same, and we are all expressing it differently. This is how those differences are carried into physical form.

As the Soul reaches down into the lower three worlds these atoms are, like all else in the universe, vibrating. They will of course, begin to attract other particles of the matter of their specific plane with an affinity to their vibratory signature. The physical manifestation of this is a single cell dividing and expanding in physical and conscious awareness until a multibillion celled organism is created... BY CONSCIOUSNESS. The Soul is a manifestation of consciousness. The mind is used by consciousness. The brain is used by the mind like the nose is used by the brain. These are the successive tools of consciousness. The nose does not know what a rose smells like, it just passes the data up the chain through the physical brain and then to the mind, which then discriminates and interprets the data. A decision is made that the data represents the presence of a rose.

When I have a thought it corresponds to chemical reactions in my head right? We are all aware at some level that the brain is a chemical and electrical mechanism. If the brain is producing the mind, as empiricists will argue, what governs the release of these chemicals? Is a random chemical release creating my thought? Or is it more likely that the thought within the mind under sub conscious, conscious, or super conscious direction, creates the chemical release as a result of the thought process. As we have seen, The Ageless Wisdom would teach that the activities of the mind precipitate downward into physical plane expression through the desire to see them materialized. As always the thought precedes the manifestation.

Incarnation

You, the spiritual essence that is you, resides in between incarnations within the Causal Body. Scripturally it is described as the Temple of Solomon. It is a temple built without hands, and we are told it must eventually (at the Fourth Initiation – See Ch. 9) be rent in two or razed to the ground. This is what happens at the end of the incarnating process but for our present discussion, the Causal Body can be considered more or less permanent.

The Soul resides in this Causal Body digesting the information acquired in the previous incarnation and preparing for the next. When the time comes, the Soul sends its probe into the world of form to gather more experience upon the physical, emotional, and mental planes. As we said before, this is much like us sending a probe into the depths of the ocean, or to a place like Mars, that we can direct through the use of radio signals to give us useful information about that environment. Now, I'm going to push this metaphor a bit, because it can carry our idea to a greater extent than some of the other's we have employed. Let's say that one of the problems we have in sending this probe, is that it loses all memory as it passes through space on its way to Mars. Some sort of electromagnetic interference erases all of the memory we put in. This is the veil of ignorance. If that stretches the imagination too far, let's just say we can't soften the bump it gets when landing. One way or another, it is artificially intelligent and capable of learning but has no memory in its databank. It arrives on Mars not knowing it's a probe or what it is there for. It begins to live for itself thinking in effect, that it's a Martian.

We are, as the creators of this probe, stuck in a waiting game. In the normal development and *learning* process, the sensitivity of its receiving equipment as well as its ability to interpret the data increases. We can then begin to send it little hints as to what we need from it but for the most part it doesn't recognize this guidance, because it doesn't recognize the source. As it gathers information on Mars we are hoping it comes up with the idea that there is some higher purpose for it being there. Who am I? What am I doing here? How did I get here? etc... If and when that happens, it decides to put up its antenna and really start listening. Bingo, we can begin to direct its actions and use this probe for its intended purpose.

With the human probe the problem is actually more complex. We have three probes to contend with and not only have they forgotten that they are probes, they are unaware of each other or even if they are aware, can be totally callous to the needs of one another. Your emotional nature, if it is the focus of your consciousness, may selfishly structure your life and control it to the detriment of the physical and or mental bodies. Eating to excess to fill some emotional need (which is impossible) can destroy the physical body. Alcohol or drug use can have the same effect. Living totally within the mind can let the body deteriorate and lead to emotional problems as well. There is a war going on inside some people over who is in charge or worse yet, its every man for himself and total chaos reigns. The person is living without intent and nothing is getting done. Now you can see the importance of what is called alignment.

So, what happens at death? The Soul withdraws its support and the organizing power having been lost, the created organism begins to die away and decompose. Life is not lost, the organizing force has simply moved on to a different task and now the form begins to disintegrate, returning the material used in its construction to the pool of matter from which it was taken, thus completing another round in the cyclic process.

This occurs in stages with the first being the dropping of the physical body. When the support of the Soul is removed, and the vital energy gone, the body lies down and begins to decompose into its component parts i.e. carbon, nitrogen etc. Ashes to ashes, dust to dust. Some people have reported seeing a spark of blue light leave the head at death but this is only the beginning of the process and that is an indication of the departure of an advanced Soul. In the average human being the point of exit is the abdomen. Cremation actually assists the withdrawal because it speeds the decomposition of the body and so aids the breakup of the etheric substance as well.

The etheric vitality has been slowly diminished over time in a person who is very ill but in the case of someone who died quickly the organs are still "alive" on this etheric level and can be used in another body, even though the Soul has departed. The fruit lives separated from the tree, alive on a cellular level, but disconnected from the vitalizing force it too will deteriorate.

With the physical body gone, the consciousness resides in the Astral Body for a time. This will vary, based on the type and strength of the Astral Body. Having a strong and even dominant astral nature is not really a good thing. If our desires were very strong in life and go unfulfilled, we can remain quite a long time in the astral world. After that, the same process occurs with the mental body, and then the Soul having finished this cycle of activity, withdraws to the causal body in a state called Devachan, or "the plane of the Gods."

Atonement or At-One-ment

So how do we get it together and get all of these bodies moving in the same direction? How do we get everything vibrating at the same pitch, so to speak? The answer is… we don't. If all is vibrating energy, then we are talking about matching the frequencies and we can't. For instance, if we slow the vibration of the Astral Body to the level of vibration on the physical plane, it would suddenly materialize. When a psychic or clairvoyant raises their vibration sufficiently, they become sensitive to and can "see" the astral body. This is actually a process of identification, because we are all functioning on all of these levels, all of the time.

That is why rather than the word align, I prefer *harmonize*. When our mind, emotions and physical nature are working in harmony, we are hitting on all 8 cylinders, to go back to the car analogy. If one of those cylinders stops firing, are we getting 7/8's of the power? No. Not only are we doing without its contribution, it is now a drag on the system.

How many times have you had the feeling of wanting what is bad for you? If you give in, who is being served? At who's detriment? We want to look out for the interests of the inner thinker, the Soul, not any one vehicle to the exclusion of the others. Now, does that mean we ignore our desires? Or for that matter the physical nature? No. There is a time and a place for everything. We just need to make sure of what our motivations are. Intent is a huge factor. It's not what you do, it's what you do. When you are in the process of a physical act, ask yourself what is motivating it. What are you really doing? When you are helping someone, are you really trying to help or are you trying to prove you don't need help? It is important because you are creating effects and resonances on planes other than the physical.

The Effects of Meditation

Mind itself is a complex subject and when we say mind it can have almost as many meanings as God. The human mind operates on different levels of expression. In the lower sub-planes of the mental plane we have the lower or *concrete mind*. On the higher plains is the creative *abstract mind*. As I alluded to earlier, one of the tasks at hand is to develop the communication link between the two. The word meditate really means to mediate. In the beginning, the goal is to mediate between the personality and the Soul and the mind is the gateway.

If we can tune the lower mind to the highest of possible thoughts we approach the level of the higher abstract mind and the flow of creativity ensues. We hear Soul influence in music. There are stories that are called "inspired." These are coming from people who have made some level of contact with the Soul. Now what about some of these creative artists who are just a screaming mess? How can someone be so troubled and so creative at the same time, if it is dependent on Soul contact?

In these cases there is simply an imbalance present. They may have developed their emotional bodies and not necessarily in a positive way, without the parallel development of the mind or the purification of the body. Its back to the wire that is incapable of handling the current applied to it. It bends and then breaks under the force. In many cases the emotional nature is just running rampant and they are flitting from one obsession to another. We relate to what they create on an emotional level and it moves us because it is so real. That makes them commercially successful but in many cases very unhappy people.

If you meditate on Kundalini for example and try to raise this force specifically or do deep breathing exercises without any guidance, you can run into real trouble. If on the other hand you develop balance in your approach through study, to sharpen and hone the mind, meditation, to link it to the Soul as well as calming the waters of the Astral Plane, and service, to foster the group awareness, Kundalini will rise at the appropriate time without any danger. It's much more fun to think of raising the serpent fire than it is to serve soup or help your elderly neighbor by shoveling his driveway but character building is an important part of the spiritual path.

CHAPTER 8

Meditation, Mystical And Occult

Now that we have an understanding of the constitution of man as a multi layered being, operating on many different planes of existence simultaneously, we are in a position to introduce the idea of Meditation into our discussion in a more meaningful way. We are going to look at meditation from a few different angles, some of the ways in which we use its practice unconsciously and what the benefits of meditation are as well. Because man is a multilayered conscious entity, the bridging of those layers through the practice of meditation can take many different forms, depending on the development and needs of the individual.

Meditation can be a simple exercise of the conscious awareness by focusing it on the physical body, in order to reach a level of relaxation. I have provided a meditation outline in Appendix A that will demonstrate this. It will relax the body and bring you into more conscious contact with it. By focusing the consciousness into different areas of the body and actively *sensing* them, we are learning to tune and direct the consciousness simultaneously. Once we become accustomed to directing our consciousness in this way, we can more easily guide it to the observance of and identification with, aspects of our selves that are not physical.

Meditation can also be used as a tool for opening up the sensitivities or a bringing down of the awareness of these sensitivities into the physical brain through the quieting and directing of the mind. If it is practiced regularly it will have a positive effect in your life. Even if it is only used sporadically, it can still affect circumstances and lead to insights. It is often associated with prayer and prayer can certainly be seen as a form of meditation. It can be guided or you can guide yourself.

The word itself is based on the Latin root medi, as in mediate. It is a bridging or mediating principle. The Christian idea of contemplation is similar. Perhaps they were uncomfortable with the mystical associations inherent with meditation and thought that word was less threatening. In the Occult Sciences, the word contemplation is reserved as an activity of the Soul. Meditation is usually associated with the Eastern religions such as the Hindu, Buddhist, and Taoist, but has application in Kabalistic teachings and Sufi practices as well. Even Jesus was described as meditating in the Garden of Gethsemane in order to square himself with his fate.

In its broadest sense it includes any type of conscious focusing of the mind or other sensitive apparatus of the personality. That which you focus upon is up to you. In its keenest sense, it is the mediating principle between the lower and higher mind and later, the Soul and Monad. In practice, it is a tuning of the consciousness to a specific vibratory range and the identification with an aspect of the self that the undeveloped man does not recognize.

This can be a useful tool in certain activities like Sports, where intruding thoughts can distract the body from doing what has been programmed into muscle memory. This technique was written about in the book *The Inner Game of Tennis*.[43] The athlete has to detach and get out of the way of her performance. Or perhaps work through some sort of injury as in the famous case of Keri Scruggs, who won the Olympic Gold Medal for her gymnastics team. She did it on the last vault of the competition,

---

[43]   W. Timothy Gallwey - *The Inner Game of Tennis: The Classic Guide to the Mental Side of Peak Performance* (New York: Random House 1974)

after not only falling but hurting her ankle on her previous vault. You could see the look on her face and the focus and determination it reflects as she goes from basically standing on one foot, to running down the lane full speed on that hurt foot and doing the vault of her life in front of billions of people. In a sense, none of us were there with her. It was just Kerry and the horse and the runway between them. Her coach had to carry her off afterward, but she did the vault and won.

Concentration like that is a form of meditation and it takes practice. Runners, cyclists and participants in any endurance sport practice this ability of conscious detachment. Excellence in these activities requires it. My brother-in-law David Yanchek can run one hundred miles. Do you think he could do that if he was not able to associate with a part of himself that does not feel pain? He and others describe a feeling of being above their body and following it, oblivious to any sensation of pain. Similar techniques can be used to focus in on some aspect of the physical body or to tune out its signals. We do this by focusing in one of the non-physical aspects of ourselves where that type of pain is not possible. This detachment can be practiced in order to lend objectivity to our response to our own problems and relationships.

These are some examples of how we can affect our physical bodies, by controlling the function of our mind with conscious intent but is that all there is? What about the other aspects of ourselves? Man is a trinity of Spirit, Soul, and body. Each of these different aspects can be seen as a triple manifestation in and of itself. Spirit, (the Monad) manifesting as Will, Love, and Activity creates the Spiritual Triad or Solar Angel, which we speak of in terms of Atma, Buddhi, and Manas. This spiritual creature dwells within the Causal Body in the upper mental planes. Then, it in its turn, it takes on the triple personality of the mental, emotional, and physical, or physio-etheric bodies.

In an undeveloped individual the personality is dominant and the Soul finds little avenue for expression on the three lower planes of human evolution. The aspects of the lower self are all running in different directions and nothing is getting done. That is referred to in the Bhagavad Gita as "inaction in action." As she develops her character, which is the first step, she begins to find it hard to justify some of her *wants* with her developing reasoning faculty and begins to allow that to hold sway, where in the beginning the physical or emotional needs dominated. In some cases, the astral or emotional nature can become so dominant that it fulfills its desires even to the detriment of others, including the other aspects of "self." This can only be controlled by the rising power of the mind in the individual.

Through character building the personality opens the door. It is integrating its physical, emotional and mental natures into a cooperative and then obviously more effective whole, and a more effective tool for the Soul. The use of physical disciplines about what to eat and how to treat the body, emotional stability and control, and the training of the mind through spiritual reading (of any sort) are the methods in this process. These practices align and develop the character of the personality and create the physical body from the finer Pranas. This will raise its vibration and its capacity to transmit the energies that are to come when she first feels the urge to meditate. Early on, meditation helps to create this balance within the personality. The integration of the personality must be accomplished to some degree before the Soul can make any real contact or exert influence in the life of the individual.

The principles to be mediated or set on rapport with each other at this point are the personality as a whole and the Soul. The gateway to the Soul is the mind and though it can be performed with devotion, meditation is a very mental practice. There are only two main divisions in which all meditations really fall, either partly or wholly. These categories can be defined as the mystical and the occult. They are closely related and most forms of meditation draw partially from both.

Bhakti Yoga or Mystical Meditation

This type of meditation is an opening of the awareness to the universe at large in what Eckhart Tolle calls "pure presence." It is the conscious raising of one's vibrations to higher frequencies and finer, subtler, energetic matter. The state of consciousness can be described as being "aware of everything and distracted by nothing." In this type of meditation we may come into contact with ideas or active communications from other forms of consciousness. It can be easy to mistake something coming from the astral plane as coming from God, or a Master. I have known of many psychics who claim they are in communication with Arch Angels. I don't know that this is true or false, but my understanding is that it would be unlikely for Arch Angels to be communicating directly with individual people. It is possible that they are receiving useful information and that the entity communicating with them is making that claim in order to make sure the information is taken seriously. It is possible that the psychic is actually creating the situation in their need to feel that they are important to the plan (a fairly common glamour). It is also possible that what they are saying is completely true. So, how do you deal with something like that? This quandary is actually easily addressed. If we only heed what is communicated when it resonates with our own understanding, then we are fairly safe from error and we are not altering our path of approach due to an illusion (on the Mental Plane) or a glamour (on the Astral Plane). This may be very useful insight that is simply not coming directly from an Arch Angel. Truth is to be heeded even if it proceeds from a monkey; just as nonsense is to be ignored even if it issues from a supposed *authority*.

Mystical Meditation is a very emotional and devotional approach, and represents the practice of Bhakti Yoga. It has a Sixth Ray resonance (the ray of devotion) and is also a very appropriate approach for what is known as the fourth sub-race of the fifth root race. It is a consciousness with ties back to the Atlantian epoch, when the emotional or Astral Body was the center of consciousness and dominant. Many people today are still functioning in what is called an Atlantian consciousness.

Meditation can be essentially self-guided with the aid of the wonderful vibrations of "singing bowls," soft music, the sound of a creek, or even silence. Experimentation in this area will reveal what is most effective for each individual. The fifth sub-race is currently in flower and expanding in the West. We are a much more mentally focused type of personality. The Fifth Ray is the ray of concrete mind and is emphasized in the sub-race because of the numerical association, which is in this case doubled. It doesn't mean Westerners are smarter. It means that we put more emphasis on mental constructs and subjugate the emotional to them. A more appropriate line of approach or the path of least resistance for most of us in the West would be: Occult Meditation.

Raja Yoga or Occult Meditation

Occult Meditation is also referred to as meditation *with seed*. The Occultist is trying to reach the same type of union with the singular force, but the motivations and methods vary. Both expand the conscious awareness and they are both effective lines of approach. Which will ultimately be the path of least resistance for an individual student depends on the student herself. The difference really lies in the focus. In one case we are dealing with an emotional polarization and the other focuses the efforts through the honing of mind. Both of these approaches are necessary for humanity as a whole and each individual student as well. The Master Djwahl Kuhl told us "The Mystic must become the Occultist and the Occultist must embrace the ways of the Mystic, if either of them is to progress upon the lighted way." Zen practice applies both of these methods in different techniques. Zazen sitting is more mystical with its emphasis on the quiet and alert mind. The student is told to "be like the frog" alert and aware through stillness. The frog is ever still, ever ready, for the moment when the fly arrives.

The more occult practice of concentration on a Kohan or riddle, which is insoluble by the concrete logical mind, provides a route to the abstract mental processes through one pointed focus or *singleness of thought*. An example of a Kohan would be "what is the sound of one hand clapping?" We must never clamp down the mind to silence it through an act of will, but simultaneously open it and free it from its incessant inner talk through this one pointed focus. As my mother used to tell me, "thine ears cannot hear, while thy tongue is wagging."

Seed thought meditation focuses the mind in a one pointed manner on a specific thought or visualization. You can meditate for instance on the word *service*, or a phrase such as "My Soul uses my mind each day in service to my fellow men." This will bring you into a new understanding of service over time and reinforce the idea of service in your mind. It will begin to permeate your thoughts outside of your meditation, first unconsciously and then later, consciously. You will begin to look at all that happens in your life as an opportunity to serve. This is the way of the Occultist. She is trying to develop her capacities in order to better serve humanity and in that way, the Plan. It should be noted that the benefits of relaxation are always present, as well as the benefits of the alignment of the personality vehicles and a development of the Will aspect through discipline. As we add new layers of meaning to the practice of meditation we multiply the benefits.

You could also meditate on selfish ends like the accumulation of riches at whatever cost. You would begin to see every circumstance as a way to amass more wealth, more personal property, and more power, in order to dominate people or direct the movements of society for selfish ends. In the creative process, white magic and black magic employ the same methods and energies. The intent is what differs. You can easily see the importance of selflessness in this context.

Sometimes the seed thought is used to provoke the imagination to the visualization of something very specific. This is another instance of what an athlete might do to enhance their performance. If the mind cannot visualize the body performing the task, how is it to *direct the body in performing that task?* If you cannot visualize yourself doing the dive, you will not do it. Jack Canfield said "You'll see it when you believe it." *Think and Grow Rich*,[44] *The Secret*, and other sources, teach this goal orientation and visualization because it works. Vision boards actually bring the idea into the physical world. The more religiously toned phrase "As a man thinketh in his heart, so is he" (Proverbs 23:7)

[44] Napoleon Hill - *Think and Grow Rich* (Cleveland, Ohio: The Ralston Publishing Co.1937)

presents the same idea. What you think about most is what you will behold in your reality.

When training in Occult Meditation we are given visualizations which are representative of what the Master knows to be the truth. The visualization is a creation in mental matter. When we visualize the lighted loving energy of the Soul pouring down and flooding the personality, we are creating that situation on the mental plane, where it is actually being brought about by this mental activity.

The Occultist uses this to gain conscious awareness and identification with his own Soul. The Soul has access to all information. It can access the Akashic Records and all of its other incarnations, as well as the wisdom gained through those experiences. It lives in the eternal now on its own plane within the Causal Body. Occult Meditation is used in the alignment of the various vehicles of the personality and in communication with the Soul. It is a scientific method of discipline, designed to open the channels of communication with the Soul through the building of the Antahkarana. Steady use of Occult Meditation will increase the flow of light through the Antahkarana and thus establish better communication with the Soul.

The Yoga Sutras of Patanjali

The Yoga Sutras of Patanjali have been translated and interpreted by many, and are available through the Lucis Trust in the book *The Light of the Soul*. It is separated into four books and is worthy of a lifetime of study. Book One deals with the problem of union. Book Two elaborates the steps to union. Book Three is titled "Union Achieved and its Results" and Book Four is simply titled "Illumination." These books lay out the successive goals of the practice alongside the techniques which will, with diligent application, bring those goals to fruition.

The Use of the OM

There are a number of reasons for the use of the OM. The Om is a very basic sound or vibration. Sound was the first act of creation in the Old Testament. The first thing God did was say "Let there be light" and he then divided the light from the darkness. We are actively cooperating with the plan as we know it when we use it in meditation.

The Mandukya Upanishad is dedicated to the meaning of the OM. It says that the Om, through its three contributing sounds A U M takes you through the seven levels of consciousness or more accurately, four states and three transitions.

The A representing the gross or Waking consciousness
The U the subtle or dreaming state
The M as the Deep Sleep state or Subconscious and the silence after the M as Samadhi[45]

In most of my reading, OM and AUM are treated as equal to one another and simply spelled in different ways. When a distinction has been drawn, the difference that has been noted is that AUM is the Destructive side of the Will aspect or "God the Destroyer," and that OM is the constructive side of that same Will aspect and more appropriate to our time and level of consciousness. Every act of creation is first an act of destruction (Picaso). The sculptor destroys a stone to release the image trapped within it. Interestingly, OM translates to *field* or, *the field*. So the meditator is acknowledging the universe as the field of play in which creation is occurring. The more unified sound OM can be seen as dominant in the refining and perfection of the creation rather than the destruction of the raw materials in the beginning of the process.

It has also been empowered for thousands of years by the millions of people by whom it has been employed. Even if it had no meaning then, it would have meaning now. When sounded aloud it has the effect of

---

[45] Samadhi has been described as a non-dualistic or unity state of consciousness in which the consciousness of the observer becomes one with the object observed.

sending vibrations through the physical and other bodies and helps to excite the etheric centers into activity and thus bridge the physical with the astral and then mental apparatus. The sound is very round and somewhat nasal, originating with the movement of the diaphragm and reverberating off of the palate. When it is used correctly it represents a breathing exercise.

I will not be giving you any breathing exercises specifically, although what I just shared with you is an enormous hint. Certain aspects of the teachings need to be related teacher to student in an environment where feedback is possible. Giving out breathing exercises where there is no ability to monitor and advise a student would be irresponsible. The other thing that I can tell you is that the visualizations and thought forms you are working with in breathing exercises are more important than the timed inhalation and exhalation of air. It is an additional tool in the awakening of consciousness but it is a powerful one and must be used carefully. Unless you are under the tutelage of someone to whom you are reporting progress, it is a good idea to stay away from them.

Group Meditation

Group Meditation is a powerful form of meditation because it uses the energy directing power of a group rather than an individual. When a group gets together for a specific purpose there is a powerful intent. Some of my most significant experiences in meditation have been in a group that meets on the full moon. It is a particularly powerful time and it is also being done around the world in every time zone. It's like a wave of good will rushing over the planet and is an overt act of service. It is an approach to the Hierarchy of the planet and an appeal for guidance and energy to flow through them into humanity via the meditators. It takes into account a keynote based on the astrological influence felt each month. More information about Full Moon and New Moon Meditations are available at LucisTrust.org.

CHAPTER 9

The Fifth Kingdom

We have posited with our First Key, the existence of one all-pervasive force in the universe and the idea that this force exists within and between all things, unobstructed and unimpeded, and that this justifies the concept of unity with all existence. We have further offered the idea that the infinite power inherent in this root principle or spiritual energy is undergoing change or evolution as it expresses itself through the manifestations of form in cyclic activity. And that consciousness is expanding into greater self-awareness through this process, called metempsychosis (alluded to in Keys Two, Three, and Four). We went on to explore that process in our discussions of the anatomy of consciousness and reincarnation. Now we are going to take a look at the longer process undergone by the Soul as it cycles through these incarnations. (Keys Five and Six)

Soul is one of the universal principles of the Trinity. It represents the middle principle of Love or Consciousness. Being universal we see it on all levels of manifestation from the simplest in the Mineral Kingdom up to the most rarified matter of the upper planes.

We are going through the process of climbing the mountain of consciousness. It is said that many vistas are available to he who has reached the mountaintop. We are now going to look at it from another angle and start at the bottom. Obviously the bottom of that mountain is the most dense and coarse form of matter and we are dealing with the Mineral Kingdom. It is here that consciousness is most encumbered, but we will see that in all Kingdoms there is an aspect of the Trinity that is predominant. We will get deeper into the Trinity in our next chapter, but it is important to note here some of the influences we see on, and through, the world around us.

In the Mineral Kingdom the focus or predominant aspect of the Trinity is Intelligent Activity. Now that may seem counter-intuitive to say the least but we have to open our minds to broader definitions of things like *mind*. I was on a philosophy forum a few years ago and someone asked if unconditional love could exist between two people. They had trouble understanding my argument, which was that whether or not unconditional love does exist, they had already placed conditions on the situation by limiting it to people. We tend to do that in the case of mind as well, by thinking we are the only ones who exhibit it. Mind is an organizing force not limited to the realm of human thought. Crystals grow in an organized fashion. Chemicals interact in predictable and repeatable ways governed by natural law. Mind, like any universal principle exists on every level of manifestation. Intelligent activity is representative of *the female principle*. Eve/Mary is female, in that it is receptive and fertile matter and overshadowed by what is religiously referred to as the Holy Ghost.

The Vegetable Kingdom is a higher expression of consciousness made up of the exact same matter we find in the Mineral Kingdom. Plants literally construct themselves with minerals using the energy of the sun. In this equation the sun represents universal Love which is the focus and predominant factor of the Trinity in the Plant Kingdom. Plants have sentience and do *feel*. Not like us, but it is love. Ask any plant person if their plants respond to love and attention. It is a higher level of consciousness and response to the environment than that of the Mineral Kingdom from which it has emerged. All human cultures use flowers intuitively to represent loving feelings. The Agni (fire) Yoga Society holds that anyone who loves flowers is "on the path of the heart."

If you want to look deeper into this idea of sentient response in the Plant Kingdom, look up the work of Cleve Backster. He used lie detectors to investigate the reactive ability of plants though a series of informal observations, as well as one completely scientific and controlled experiment. In this experiment live brine shrimp were dumped into boiling water by an automated machine with no human presence. Plants placed in three adjacent rooms reacted immediately and simultaneously to their destruction. In one of his most interesting observations plants reacted to the thought of being burned before a match was lit. After a number of repetitions, individual plants *realized* there was in fact no danger, and the reactions subsided. Repeating the process with a new plant repeated the original results, including this realization over time of the absence of any real danger.

In the Animal Kingdom we have added to those two qualities the first tangible expression of a Will. There is mind and even reason, as well as love in a much higher form of expression but now the Will is the focus of consciousness. Animals move and extend themselves to a purpose in a manner beyond what we see in the lower kingdoms. This is seen in the Plant Kingdom as well, in the form of the impetus that drives the seedlings roots down into the soil and its leaves up into the light of the sun, but now it is the dominant factor.

So, we have all three aspects of the Trinity expressed through the lower Kingdoms. Now as we move into the fourth or Human Kingdom, all are expressed in their highest forms yet. We feel love consciously, and we are capable of willing and acting with full awareness as well. We have come full circle and find ourselves back to the principle of mind, or Intelligent Activity. The dominant aspect of man is that we are creatures of mind. We overcome our relatively frail physical nature and all obstacles to our survival through the exercise of that mind. It is expressed on a higher turn of the spiral but is this as far as it goes? Are we to consider ourselves to be the last stage in the evolution of consciousness through form? Can we possibly answer that question in the affirmative and still claim to believe in God? I don't think so.

There is another Kingdom we have seen evidenced throughout our history right here on earth. The need for a dramatic physical change in this case just doesn't exist, so in one sense we see these beings as our peers. At the same time, we recognize them as powerful beyond our abilities and in some cases beyond our ability to imagine. Of course I speak of the likes of Lao Tsu, Moses, Jesus, and others who have been described as having entered the Kingdom of God, or Heaven. Those who have achieved Nirvana, Satori, or as it is called in the West, Enlightenment or Illumination. To these religious figures I would add Pythagoras, Socrates, Plato and Aristotle, and even Mozart, Da Vinci, Emerson, and Francis Bacon. These are giants among men in every area of human endeavor. All are unique and different like humans are all different. What they have in common is that they have travelled the path consciously, where the rest of humanity is evolving unconsciously in comparison. They have taken their evolution into their own hands and in so doing, accelerated the process. This transition or transformation is described in great detail in the book Cosmic Consciousness. It is also detailed as it applies to all of humanity in my Father's book The Christ Epoch,[46] but an outline of the common steps bears mention here.

In the beginning the human consciousness is outward in its focus. Food, comfort, sex, and the various survival drives govern most of our activity. These are drives we share with the Animal Kingdom. We can see (with the exception of the sexual urge) that we grow through this stage as we mature from infancy and childhood, where our concern is only for our own needs and desires, into a more mature outlook that includes the family and we learn to share. This growth in the circle of influence begins to include the school, town and later the country in which we live. As we learn to identify ourselves as part of these larger and larger groups, we begin to see ourselves as more than what we first perceived. We begin to consciously look at who we are and why we are doing what we are doing. Your reading of this book is an indication that you have reached at least this stage in the process of spiritual awakening.

---

[46] Anthony J. Fisichella - *One Solitary Life – Book III: The Christ Epoch* (USA: Authorhouse 2008)

At this point you are referred to in the occult philosophies as an "Aspirant." You are aspiring to something greater and acknowledge that you are not there yet. As an aspiring actor looks and works toward a successful career, you aspire to a greater knowledge of yourself, and so do I. Even the Master fits this definition in his own way, so there is no egotism in referring to yourself in this manner.

As the Aspirant starts to become aware of the conscious nature of her being, she begins to turn toward that aspect of herself. Note those words. Consciousness and awareness are synonyms. She is becoming aware of being aware. As a matter of fact, she is on the path to the awareness that her true nature is pure awareness, so as she treads this path she is becoming aware of her *self* in its essence. As she approaches the Soul and comes into an ever increasing level of contact with that higher aspect of herself through identification, this interaction begins to show as aspiration towards a different type of life. Her desire is now to express a more clear representation of the higher self.

This causes conflict between the old ways deeply ingrained in the personality and the new rhythm of living and set of values trying to express themselves in her everyday life. She goes from high on the mountain top down to the valley of despair as if on a roller coaster ride. The only way to survive is to find within herself a disciplined nature that can control and direct to positive ends the influx of this new energy in her life.

At this point the Aspirant has taken the step towards a disciplined and focused life of study, meditation, and service. By far the most important of these is service. She is now the Disciple on the path of holiness. The only real difference between the Aspirant and the Disciple is a level of commitment. Every Disciple is an Aspirant. She has established a new rhythm in her life and much of that early conflict has passed. The higher self has become a fact in her life. She subjects herself to disciplines with which the average person is not concerned or of which they are not even aware. She is treading the Tao or "Way" consciously now.

She will eventually come under the guidance of another disciple or initiate who is ahead of her on the path and later, the scrutiny of a

Master or Adept; one of humanity's guides. A Master has answered to the call of "Be ye therefore perfect even as your father in heaven is perfect." (Matt. 5:48) The "father in heaven" is a reference to the Monad, or individuated spark of the divine flame, just as the "golden bowl" of the Old Testament is a reference to the Soul, and she reflects that perfection in every aspect of the lower self or personality.

There is a further stage referred to as Accepted Discipleship that describes the acceptance by the Master on your Ray[47] and admittance into his Ashram. At this point she will likely be schooled in her astral body while the physical body sleeps between 10:00pm and 5:00am. She is serving the plan through group effort along with her spiritual brothers. This process spans many incarnations as she is training and disciplining herself, failing and succeeding, until she reaches the portal of initiation, by self-devised and self-induced methods. She has now made herself worthy and enters a new process in her evolution.

She is leaving the Hall of Learning and entering the Hall of Wisdom. Adam and Eve represent the exit from the Hall of Ignorance into the Hall of Learning. This is symbolic of the individualization that separates animal man from the human conscious entity we see in ourselves. Now she is being "born anew" into the Kingdom of Heaven, and is ready for the first of five Initiations that will mark the path into this new world of experience.

Initiation

All of this discipline, and the process of awakening that it brings about, represent a step by step entry into the Fifth Kingdom of Nature through a series of what are called "Initiations." This is the hidden subject of the New Testament as it follows Jesus through the process of his awakening into the Christ nature. Remember our Seventh Key, spiritual knowledge is always given in symbolic terms. That idea will be

---

47 See Chapter 11 for a full explanation of the Masters and the Ashrams of The Seven Rays.

illustrated repeatedly through this section. The First Initiation is called the Birthing Initiation. The Disciple must be born anew in order to enter the Kingdom of God. The Christ Principle in each and every one of us is the Soul or "hope of glory." (Col 1:27)

Soul and Son are synonyms. We each must give birth to that (Christ) principle in our hearts. At this stage we continue to function in our personality and we will move over time into a better expression of the Soul. At that time the personality is no longer expressing itself, it is expressing the Soul. It is a question once again of what part of the self is the focus. What it is within this complex self with which we identify. This leads us from what is known as the Hall of Learning into:

The Hall of Wisdom – The Promised Land, Heaven, Mecca, Nirvana, or Satori

Is there any among us who really believe that we will enter a physical place as symbolically represented by these words? Is there a Hall of Wisdom or a place called Heaven? I propose that in each case we are dealing with a symbolic statement of a new level consciousness; a state of mind or more accurately, *being*. "The Kingdom of God is within you," we are told (Luke 17:21). How can this be interpreted in any other way? We are now speaking of the Fifth Kingdom of Nature and as we repeated the aspect of Intelligent Activity in man, we repeat the emphasis of Love in this new kingdom. Christ is called the "Lord of Compassion" and preached Love rather than Law. Buddha said he felt the whole world's woes but rejoiced in the knowledge of liberation. The process of initiation is the path to this liberation.

The word initiation represents a new beginning as much as it does the completion and accomplishment of the purposes of the previous order of work. It consummates as well but the primary concern is with what lies ahead. It is like the commencement ceremony at the graduation from one level of academic achievement into the next, or the entry into the world as a practitioner of your particular type of expertise. They say that today is the first day of the rest of your life, and the Aspirant has gone from the Path of Probation to that of Discipleship and now enters upon the Path of Initiation. This again is simply a new stage in the process. She will now demonstrate power over the appetites of the flesh and begin to address those astral desires that are unrelated to survival in any way, like the accumulation of stuff. She hears what her body wants and only listens if and when it is prudent to do so. She desires only to serve and knows that her basic needs will be met if she does so selflessly. The wealth that will inevitably come into her life will be used for the expansion of her work and not her worth, for she does not see worth in the same way. Most people are running around unconscious of how they are reacting to their environment in a sort of *override mode* which is either emotional or worse yet, survival based.

The Disciple and now Initiate is becoming increasingly aware of being aware. She begins to unfold a tremendous sense of self, but not in the way we usually use that term, which is to indicate the separated or personality nature. She is becoming aware of the unity of all things and is working in the world of meaning. She is becoming more able to ascertain the underlying meaning of the events in her life and what is working for her, as well as what is not.

The Initiations

The First Initiation – The Birthing – Earth

The First Initiation represents a birth of physical purity and is symbolized by Virgin Birth in Christianity, as well as many of the other world religions. The Disciple will only be aware of the fact that she is an initiate if it happened in this life time. If not, she will have retained the qualities of consciousness that are necessary to further her development but will have to unfold and get in touch with them again. Many of you on the spiritual path may have already undergone this initiation in a previous cycle or incarnation.

The Second Initiation – The Baptism – Water

The First is identified with earth for obvious reasons. It is the most physical and dense of what are known as the four elements. It represents the redemption and control of the physical form. The Second Initiation is associated with water. This too makes sense if you recall our conversation about the astral nature and the associations with liquid as well as weather metaphors. The Astral Plane is known also as the Cosmic Liquid Plane and represents the next level of energetic substance in the realm of human evolution. We are now concerned with the purification and control of the emotional body.

The Second Initiate has now shown her ability to override the dictates of the flesh, and the emotional needs as well. Emotional desires transcend any reasonable need, like wealth for its own sake. It may seem like a need but that is because of the orientation of the consciousness involved. You cannot live without food. You can live without the Cadillac. It may just seem like you can't.

Further, the Second Initiate has lost the ability to hurt with words. She leads a harmless lifestyle, sensitive to the impact she has on her fellow men. She is not prone to the kind of angry outburst or roller coaster of feelings that the early Aspirant on the path may experience. The body has been purified, and this is an essential step to emotional stability. Without the toxins contained in highly processed or inappropriate foods, the emotional nature is more easily stabilized. We talk of precipitation from the more rarified levels down to the more dense but the lower vehicle must be prepared for this influx of energy or disaster results. The lower nature must be pure in order to accurately reflect the higher. She is steady of heart and committed to the path she travels.

The Third Initiation – The Transfiguration – Air

The Third Initiation is known as the first of the major initiations. It is associated with the element of air because it regards the purification and control of mind. Further it is considered the first of the major initiations because it is the final step in the purification and integration of the personality as a whole. Consciousness at this level is sometimes referred to as "Cosmic Consciousness" or better termed "causal" consciousness. She has causal awareness of the higher mental planes. At the third Initiation she will achieve full continuity of consciousness and will be aware of the activities in which she participates when her physical body sleeps. It is the initiation of the mind, but just as importantly it represents the total integration of the personality or lower self and the full recognition of the personality as a vehicle of self, rather than its identity. She has now achieved the balance of the energy of all three of her personality vehicles and has integrated them into a unified perfected whole and knows that this is not the essence of herself. She knows now that she is an Initiate and always will. She is aware of all of her incarnations without the need to read the Akashic Records. She is by every measure of humanity a perfected individual and now she is to surrender that individuality to the whole.

The Fourth Initiation - The Great Renunciation or Crucifixion – Fire

A wealthy man was advised by Jesus that in order to enter the Kingdom he should sell all he had, give to the poor, and follow him, but could not at that time. He was not ready to renounce the riches that he had acquired in his life. He was attached to things that "dust and moth doth corrupt." (Mathew 6:29) Jesus also stated in Mathew 19:24 that it was easier for a camel to pass through the eye of a needle, than it is for a rich man to enter the Kingdom. This is not a slam on rich people but a statement of the impossibility, at this point on the path, to remain attached to the objects of the physical plane.

This refers not only to gold and silver but all of the possessions on the physical, astral, and mental planes. As we will see in more detail during our discussion of the seven planes of manifestation, this also includes the Causal Body, which is the first vehicle of the Soul. It is symbolized by the Temple of Solomon and is the temple that was "rent in twain from the top to the bottom" (Mathew 27:51) as Jesus hung on the cross.

There is no Temple on Mount Golgotha. There is no way to interpret this statement outside of symbolism.

In order to fully enter the Kingdom she must surrender and raze to the ground Solomon's Temple. It has served her well but is no longer necessary as she prepares to ascend to monadic consciousness; the "father in heaven." This is total dis-identification with all things within the Human Kingdom. You literally can't take it with you. Christ did not ascend in a human physical body. He lays it at the feet of God In sacrifice. Most of us think of sacrifice as the giving up of something in order to get something else. The real meaning of the word is "to make sacred." The Causal Body is burned up by the electric fire of Spirit and the Initiate becomes aware of her true essence as an individualized spark of the "all-consuming fire" that is God.

The Fifth Initiation – The Ascension

She is now a Master, an Adept or Mahatma (great self or Soul). These are "the just men (*people*) made perfect." (Hebrews 12:23) St. Paul tells us that Christ is the "eldest of many brethren" (Romans 8:29). An honor by any measure but inconsistent with the idea of the only begotten son. These are the members of the Spiritual Hierarchy or government of the planet. They are masters of themselves, not of others. They are Masters of The Seven Rays or great modifications of energy that we will discuss in detail in Chapter 11.

Technically she still produces Karma but there is nothing in her being that would produce a negative effect. Remember, Karma is not punitive or bad. It is totally neutral and impersonal. She has proven herself totally harmless and so, trusted with great power because she won't do any damage with it. The triplicity of Spirit, Soul and body is gone and now a duality remains; literally the Spirit and form with no intermediary necessary.

At this stage she is capable of manifesting her will spontaneously, a power known in Sanskrit as Kriashakti. There is no need to resurrect the physical body because she can create a perfect one with the power of her will. The most celebrated occurrence of this is the resurrection of the Christ after his crucifixion, but it leaves an open question in the Christian interpretation. If Jesus did resurrect and repair the same physical vehicle after his perceived death on the cross, then Mary Magdalene would have recognized him immediately as her Master when she came upon him in the Garden. (John 20:14) He warned her not to touch him when she did have the realization of who he was. What reason would there be if he had simply brought his physical form back to life as he had done with Lazarus? (John 11)

The powers of clairvoyance, the spontaneous manifestation of the Will and the ability to transcend time and space to live in the eternal now; these are the things that evolution into the Fifth Kingdom of nature produce. It is the path to mastery of the self and the true understanding and application at will of the Laws of Nature.

The Threefold Path

There are other initiations called the initiations of Decision and Resurrection which go well beyond the intended scope of this work and I will posit that they are significantly beyond the steps with which we, as human beings, need concern ourselves. So, what are those steps? What is it that we can do at this stage of our evolution in order to take it consciously in hand?

The path is said to consist of three central activities coordinated and focused within the mind, heart, and activity of the student of spiritual science. The first is study. Study of philosophy, scripture, mathematics, and or anything else of a higher nature is the first step. Additionally, it is learning how to live as a more effective human personality. This is the work of the various motivational and human potential disciplines. Of course there is a multi-layered effect if we study works directly written about the journey but anything that hones the mind is of help. Learn the alphabet of the path. That is what you are doing here.

The next step but not in a temporal sense necessarily, is to meditate and reach for an understanding of what you study. Open yourself to the intuition of the Soul. Find the inner thinker or witness through meditation or *mediation*. The mind is the gateway to higher consciousness and it is the mental plane on which the Rainbow Bridge or Antahkarana is to be built. When we visualize our goals we set up a form of tension that brings them closer to us.

The last and perhaps most important step is to serve and help your brothers and sisters on the lighted way. Teach, write or sing, paint, or just help in a shelter. This brings into a personal experience the fact of our unity. Share. Otherwise you have no outlet for the energy coming into your life and you will have problems and hold yourself back. Charity is selfish in that it brings to the charitable more joy than those she serves, if she does so selflessly. Serve for the sake of those you help, not for the rewards or accolades you may receive and your service will change your consciousness, which will change your life. This change in your life and the example it brings to others can be the most effective service you can render. The universe has no choice but to respond to our actions; good, bad or indifferent. Just as the air has no choice but to carry the sound of your voice. You set up a vibration and the environment resonates and carries it to the inevitable conclusion. As a student of the mysteries you have a choice as to what you will create. That is the level of your free will.

The Student

The Christ will return and the presence of these many teachers and this entire movement is in preparation for that moment but how do you conduct yourself with these great spiritual leaders and teachers? What is the proper attitude of the student in the presence of a Master or even his teachers on the physical plane?

An important thing to remember is that a sapling cannot grow in the shadow of a great oak. Live life and be aware. Do not live in the shadow of some guru trying to become enlightened by proxy or osmosis. Think for yourself. This is the path of the Occultist. Learn from everyone and take nothing as fact just because of its source. No one can better decide what is true than you. You will not become an initiate by clinging to the coat-tails of a Master. You will not gain the attention of a Master by worshiping him either. If you wish to gain admittance into the inner mysteries you must show them that you are useful. The Masters are servants of Humanity. If you want to help them with their work all you need to do is serve humanity. They do not see what you do as much as they see the light you radiate, so work on your attitude of gratitude and help those around you in any way you can.

There is a simple Mantra you can say every morning to help yourself along the path. It can keep you moving forward with the right perspective. It is "Today I will function as intelligently, as wisely, and lovingly, as I know how." Notice that when I say this I am not comparing my behavior to that of the Master, or of any other student. I am working on myself and hopefully tomorrow when I say it I will be a little better at it (at being me).

The Master

So if that is the attitude of the student then what can be said of the Master? The first and perhaps most interesting fact is that they do not demand obedience. They suggest a course that they see as being beneficial and then allow you to determine your path and grow by those "self-devised and self-induced methods." The student must embark upon and travel the path of his own free will. If you are hearing a demand of strict adherence to doctrine or dogma by a teacher at any level you are dealing with a personality and probably an insecure one. This is not the behavior of someone who is enlightened. You may want to consider moving on but it is your call. Remember the words of the Buddha and don't believe a thing that is said just because it is said by a Master or a teacher or sage. It is up to you to determine at every step of the way what is true, good and useful for you at your stage of development. If it rings true, act on it and do so abundantly.

From the Tao comes the one
From the one comes the two
From the two comes the three
From the three comes myriad things

Lao Tsu – The Tao te Ching

CHAPTER 10

The Enigma Of The Trinity

If you perform your own investigation you will find this concept central to almost every religious teaching you encounter. It is characterized in different ways, but the concept of the One Life differentiated into the multiplicity of being is the basis for most belief systems. A supreme creator of all is followed and assisted by leagues of deific forces guiding the manifested world in expression. Whether this is a Pagan scheme with many Gods and elemental forces or a monotheistic one which talks of a single God with Angels and Demons, there is one creative energy or entity characterized as central to all and then various degrees of lesser "Gods" or forces bringing forth the world we know and guiding or beguiling us as we learn and grow. One Life, many forms of expression and the first and second of our keys are reflections of this widely held truth. As a matter of fact, it is in this section where you will see clearly all of the keys that I have articulated, coming together and embodying the creation of the universe. It is in this symbolic representation that we see the One Life, manifest as the many, through the interaction of spiritual essence, vivifying matter, as a result of vibration, in successive cycles, and ever widening spirals. The emergent levels of conscious expression reflect this creative act, above and below.

One represents the unity of all life; the one root principle and infinite power that pervades the universe. This is usually termed God, a synonym of God, or a name assigned to a being or force whose description fits the definition of God where attempts are made at defining it. It is the ultimate abstraction or "The One Life" that is the cause of all manifestation. We are all in this together because we are "cut from the same bolt of cloth."[48] Life is the source of all, but how does this differentiation occur?

In order to explore this abstract process, we will have to invoke symbolism because we are trying to project an idea that cannot be communicated directly. It can only be experienced directly. This, as we have discussed, is the reason for religious symbolism. In The Book of Genesis, the first differentiation from this state of total unity is the separation of light from the darkness. We start of course with the undifferentiated whole. It is a sea of pure potential referred to in Sanskrit as mulaprakriti. In a sense it is like a thermodynamic system at equilibrium, waiting for perturbation. A spark of an idea is what happens first, and in this case the result is the entire manifested universe. At every level it is true that energy follows thought. It was a thought in the mind of this infinite awareness that I jokingly phrase as "wouldn't it be cool if there was light?" The idea is formed into the words which are then sounded forth. Vibration is the basis of all manifestation. Sound is used to symbolize vibration, and it comes second. Remember we are dealing with symbols. There was no physical being there to sound forth the word. There was really no "there" there, to serve as an environment for a physical being to inhabit or an atmosphere to carry the "sound".

In the story, God says "Let there be light." This is a powerful mantram that brings about the first differentiation of this pre-existent proto-matter. The articulation of the idea is the first creative act itself and the thought form is crystalized on the Mental Plane as symbolized by the light of mind. For the first time we have light and darkness or *duality*

---

[48]   In colonial times, when cloth and fabrics were often purchased in bulk to make clothing for an entire family, the family was considered to be **cut from the same bolt of cloth**.

and we are now in the beginnings of the manifested universe. Creation is the result of action taken, based on the desire to see an idea crystalized and made into a reality.

Manifestation requires this duality. Every top has a bottom. Insides always come with outsides and they define each other. As we discussed earlier on, when we define something, we create a duality. What it is and what it is not, but there is an instantaneous third, which is the relationship between the two. All things are relative. Good does not exist without evil. Why? Because without evil in contrast good is meaningless. Without light to define it, darkness is meaningless. Electricity is always measured from a reference point; positive means nothing without negative. You can have a million volt battery but you cannot get power from the plus side unless the minus side is connected. As a matter of fact, the power comes from the minus side in the form of the movement of the negatively charged electrons toward the positive potential at the other pole. This gives you an idea about how deep our misunderstandings go and where we started. We will need to shelve this awkward idea of electrical polarity because it will confuse the issue, so for our purposes here we will simply stay with the conventional use of these terms.

God, or as Lao Tzu described it, "the subtle essence of the universe" is neither positive nor negative, perfect nor imperfect (good or evil) but the source of both. It is truly the essence of both and the totality from which they are derived. Thus we live in a relative world of relative truth, which is the result of this initial split into duality, caused by vibration. This duality automatically creates a trinity because of the relationship between the polar opposites. The top is only the top because of where the bottom is. We are going to look at this Trinity in a number of different ways, because that will help illustrate this relationship. It is the most important aspect of what we are addressing.

The basic formula for creation can be represented mathematically in the equation 1+2=3. Now, you may ask why I did not start with what would seem to be the most basic math equation 1+1=2. There is a difference between the first and this second equation in that in the second a quantity is increased but nothing new has been created. If I have one molecule of Hydrogen (the simplest atom) and add another, I simply have more hydrogen. If I have one molecule of oxygen and two molecules of hydrogen, combining them will create something new, water. Two separate conditions with an affinity for each other combine to create a new condition, which is the result of that affinity or relationship. Man plus man and I have men. Man plus woman and I have creation, or more accurately the formula for creation that is represented *and reflected* in the symbolism of the Trinity.

In this personified version male is considered positive because he posits, not because he is good. The name Joseph means "one who will add" and interestingly, he was a carpenter or builder. Female is considered negative in the sense that she is receptive, not bad. Of course we know that man posits and woman receives. This personification of the aspects of the unified creative force, and its interrelationship in the dualistic manifested world has given birth (if I may use such an obvious play on words) to many misconceptions. Spirit, in the words of the Bhagavad Gita "pervades matter with a fragment if itself and yet remains." God is seen as a personified male entity by many but that is a fundamental error at the outset, because the source pre-exists creation in the un-manifest state. Polarity does not exist at this stage and comes into being with the advent of the material world. God cannot be the result of creation and the creator simultaneously, so the causeless cause that precedes the existence of male/ female, light/dark, or plus/minus, must be seen as creator (God) and devoid of this differentiation. Therefore male is not more divine than female as they are two sides of a duality on which they are mutually dependent for their existence.

In our example above, the creation of water or more accurately the re-organization of the hydrogen and oxygen atoms into water does not destroy either. They create, and yet remain. This is true even in the case of heavier molecules created in the furnaces of the universe. The sun has been seen as the creator or God of our solar system since before we understood it, and in this sense the stars or suns are the creators. In the first moments following the big bang, nothing existed, other than hydrogen and then helium. Helium is created under the immense pressure of gravity within the star by combining four hydrogen atoms. This combination actually releases energy in the form of heat and light, which is why stars shine. The rest of us can exist because of the life giving and sustaining power of this light and heat. Every molecule in the universe heavier than hydrogen was created in a star. They are truly the creators of the physical world. "We are Stardust, we are golden. We are billion years old carbon" as we are told in the popular song by Crosby, Stills and Nash, and they further advise us to "get ourselves back to the garden," or our source. There is more to the worship of the sun than the idea that it was just a big scary ball in the sky above the heads of the early races of humanity that they were too unsophisticated to understand. It makes more sense than much of what we collectively believe today.

Spirit/Matter/Consciousness

One of the characterizations of this Trinity is that of spirit or the male principle vivifying matter, the female principle. The result of this interaction is consciousness. The cross, which it seems, is rarely to be seen in Christian tradition without Jesus hanging from it, actually predates Christianity by thousands of years. The earliest symbols referred to in the Secret Doctrine's analysis of the ancient Stanzas of Dzyan are the circle (as we discussed, a symbol for the universe) followed by a circle with a dot in the center, signifying the stirring and awakening of the universal deity. The third is a circle with a horizontal line bisecting it (spirit at the top/ matter, at the bottom), now a duality. The fourth is the circle with a second bisecting line at a 90 degree angle to the first, forming a cross in the circle. This is the symbol for the result of the duality created by Spirit and matter or *consciousness*. The cross actually represents the Trinity of Spirit, Soul or consciousness, and matter. In cases like the Rose Cross and the symbol of the Golden Dawn, a rose or other flower is placed at the center to indicate the flowering of consciousness as a result of this interaction.

Let's take another look at this interrelationship from a different angle, if you will pardon another pun. Picture a right triangle which (by definition) has one 90 degree angle, with the vertical side labeled "A" the base labeled "B." The Hypotenuse is "C" which forms the third side and is the result of the relationship of the A side to the B side. If we change A we also change C because it is born of the relationship, but B may be left unchanged. If we change B but not A, C still changes. Now replace the names. A is Spirit. – B is matter – C is consciousness, born of the interaction of the two. It evolves because of the interaction. We cannot evolve without form and we cannot be conscious without form, as fine as the matter of that form may be. Consciousness, as the relationship between form and the spiritual essence that brings it to life, is affected by both the essence, and the form it inhabits. They are all in fact interactive and a change in consciousness will affect the material of the form. The spiritual essence is also affected and evolves in the process as well. As we mentioned before, the whole system evolves.

This Trinity represents the three latent Principles or the "Aspects" of Divinity. In the Theosophical literature they are termed Will, Love, and Intelligent Activity or Active Intelligence. They are symbolically represented in many ways through religious scripture but these three words correlate to those symbols very closely in the thinking of the Western mind. I am going to take them one at a time and show you what I mean.

The first aspect is Will. It is the driving force in the system. This is the force that drives the seedling up out of the ground, as well as what gets you out of bed in the morning. The stirring of this will to create brought into activity that great slumbering force described so poetically in the book of Genesis. This is the precursor to the idea and is represented by the dot in the circle. It is the will to *be* when nothing yet *was*.

The third aspect is Active Intelligence or adaptability, and represents the field of play. This field is the pre-matter which is described in Genesis as "the deep." It is the potential matter, not yet vivified by that creative will. This is the quantum field of particle physics and the "mulaprakriti" of Sanskrit. It is pure un-manifest potential which responded to that initial vibration when God uttered the creative word (Logos) and all came into being. This is nature, which is responsive to the will aspect and spontaneously comes into *being* based on that vibratory signature of the word of power to which it is responding. The word and the Will are the same, but without the deep nothing is created. Male is not more important than female.

The second aspect is Love, and I skipped it because if timing was involved, this middle principle would have to be considered to come last, as it is the result of the interaction of the other two. This creative process exists in a realm outside of time so that is actually a misconception, based on our finite ability to reason. Another term used in describing this middle principle is consciousness but in a manner that we may not be accustomed to considering. We are not talking about human consciousness alone or the mere sense of being awake. An amoeba is a conscious living entity responding to its environment and so is the atom of oxygen as it combines with the hydrogen to form water. This bond can be broken if a particle with a stronger affinity is presented. It may steal away the oxygen atom leaving the hydrogen high and dry. (Okay, I'll stop with the puns)

There is another way to look at this and I think you will begin to see how these terms never suffice individually but when all are taken into account an abstract vision of truth begins to emerge. The trinity can be seen as Life, Quality, and Appearance. Life is the constant (if there is a constant) like the Will. It is that driving force. I am both amused and horrified by the abortion and contraception controversies that are manufactured for political ends in this country; the debate about life, and whether it begins at conception or implantation in the uterus etc. When did life begin? I want to know when they think it ended. The sperm and egg are both alive and neither is human but they were created *alive* inside a human. I believe the same of the zygote, the embryo, and the fetus, as well as the entire physical body. None are human. They are merely the successive stages in the building of a vehicle that the *human being* will inhabit, for as long as it remains useful. Then it will be dropped and what is human will move on.

The body represents the outer appearance. Appearance is the outward manifestation of the life force and the interaction of the two is the

Quality. Life is life, whether it manifests in the form of a man or a tree. Life is pure being – manifested forms are *qualified* expressions of life. The life of a tree reflects a different quality than the life in me, but in its pure essence it is the same. We are both alive. I am a finite expression of an infinite force of nature. As I unfold that life within myself to a greater degree, I approach ever more closely to that unqualified purity. The evolutionary drive toward perfection is an expression of life itself and is inevitable.

We can also say Life – Consciousness – Form. Life manifesting through form creates consciousness. Life manifesting through different forms results in a differing quality of expression or consciousness. We have said that man consists of Spirit, Soul and Body. The spiritual essence of man being identical with that of the rest of the universe, on the path to self-awareness, reflects the creative process in its own system. It creates a form and inhabits it consciously. The relationship between Spirit and Body produces Soul or consciousness. We are the same Life in a similar Form with the alteration being our consciousness.

Man is known as the microcosm with relation to the macrocosm, represented by the always inadequate term, God. We talked about the ways this trinity is reflected through the constitution of the human being and the various forms of which it consists. The personality consists of mind, emotions, and physical body, a reflection of the aspects of Will, Love, and Activity on the lower planes. This can be pictured as an equilateral triangle pointed down. The Soul is a trinity of Spiritual Will – Intuition (Love) and - Abstract or creative mind. This is pictured as a triangle with the point up.

St. Paul said of Jesus, "He made in himself of twain, one new man." (EPH 2:15) This is the merging of these two trinities; and these interlaced triangles form the symbol of the six pointed star. Then if the tenth letter of the Hebrew alphabet, the yod (The "I" representing that original spiritual impulse in the microcosm) is placed in the middle we have seven. Three is the number of creation and seven is the number of manifestation. When merged with the original Trinity (God) this gives us ten, the number of perfection and a representation of re-union with the divine in consciousness.[49] We merge the lower self with the higher self and then with the unity or source. This is the purpose of evolution. It is the evolution of consciousness and all we see is merely an effect of that ongoing process.

Some examples of this trinity from other religious systems are Shiva – Vishnu – Brahma from the Hindu traditions, Kether – Chokma – Binah (Hebrew) or Atma – Buddhi – Manas (Buddhism). You will see as we progress, and through your other readings, that the Ageless Wisdom teachings draw much of their influence and terminology from the Buddhist traditions, which use the Sanskrit terms none of us really like to get into. This is partly because there are no English words that correlate directly to these terms. For me, this ends up being both the reason to use the Sanskrit words and the reason no one wants to.

Below there are some correlations that may help you to clarify the principles involved. In the creative process we see the concept of the conscious entity or the knower, interacting with the field of knowledge as:

The Knower – Knowing – The Known

(Unchanging) – (Mutable) – (Also unchanging, just re-arranged)

As a universal principle would be, we see the reflection of this idea in every creative act.

In Art

The Artist – Masterpiece – Clay

In Government

The will of the people – The administration of law - The laws created

---

[49] In the practice of numerology, one and ten are seen as the same, implying that God and its creation are one.

In Religion

Esoteric Teachings – Fundamental Symbolism – Outer doctrine

In Education

The will to learn – The arts and sciences – The structure of the educational system

Some further examples upon which you can ponder or meditate.

ENERGY	AWARENESS	SUBSTANCE
TAMAS	SATVA	RAJAS
INERTIA	RHYTHM	MOBILITY
STABILITY	HARMONY	VIBRATION
SPIRIT	SOUL	BODY
MONAD	EGO	PERSONALITY
DIVINE SOUL	HUMAN SOUL	ANIMAL SOUL
THE POINT	THE TRIAD	THE QUATERNARY
WHAT IS	WHAT KNOWS	WHAT DOES
FATHER	SON	HOLY GHOST

CHAPTER 11

Esoteric Psychology –
The Study Of The Seven Rays

Through all of our discussion we have maintained the existence of a single unified force that permeates the entire manifested universe on all the varied planes of existence. This force can be seen as expressing itself through seven interrelated qualities and they, in their totality, the unified force. The use of color to describe the filtering or distortion of an idea or situation is an intuitive recognition of these qualities of expression and each is associated with a color of light. Color relates to the frequency of light radiation, from the infra-red at the bottom of the spectrum, to the ultra-violet at the high end. Here we have another example of the rate of vibrations determining the differentiation of expression of this life force.

These differentiated rays of energy are seven in number and are, of course, referred to as The Seven Rays. The study of these qualities of expression is also known as Esoteric Psychology, for reasons that will become apparent as we proceed. It has a practical application, but we are going to get more esoteric on this subject than any we have covered thus far. Psychology is considered the study of the mind but it is really the study of the Soul or more accurately "Soul." Psyche means Soul, and the suffix –"ology" indicates that it is *the knowledge of,* so psychology is really the knowledge of the Soul, or consciousness aspect. *Esoteric* as we have discussed, refers to the inner or causal meaning rather than the outer expression. So, what we are going into is a deeper understanding of consciousness and its expression in the worlds of evolution. What does that have to do with Rays? In order to get to that logically we are going to have to back up a bit.

In the beginning... I'm not kidding; we have to go to the beginning. We have posited the existence of this all pervasive force in the universe and the idea that this force exists within and between all things, unobstructed and unimpeded, and that this is the justification for the concept of unity with all existence. We have further offered the idea that the infinite power inherent in this root principle or spiritual energy is undergoing change or evolution as it expresses itself through the manifestations of form, in cyclic activity and that consciousness is expanding into greater self-awareness through this process, called metempsychosis. We went on to explore that process of metempsychosis as it relates to the human consciousness where it is termed reincarnation, as well as the longer process undergone by the Soul as it cycles through these incarnations. Then we looked at the Kingdoms of Nature and how we as humans (the fourth Kingdom) are evolving into the fifth Kingdom and the initiatory process that governs the transformation.

The story of creation, no matter where it is found, always starts with one single pre-existent being, force, or intelligence. This level of consciousness is so refined that we can't even conceive its nature. He (*or it.. or that*) is referred to in the esoteric classics as "He about whom naught can be said" because this entity or Life Force is so far beyond the capability of the human mind to conceive. This is a God of no name or an entity into whose face we cannot look. At this point it does not matter what term we use to describe it for the term is an attempt to define the indefinable and so, must fall short. Rather than Allah, Lord or God we could append the equally inappropriate name of Fred or even "X."

Issuing from this exalted being are seven rays of energy. The totality of existence differentiated for the first time by the variance in vibrational frequency alone, expressing various qualities of that totality while never being divided from it. If this is sounding familiar it is because the three

Aspects of Divinity we discussed in the chapter on the Trinity are in fact the first three rays. Then the Third Ray of Intelligent Activity is subdivided into what are known as four "Attributes of Divinity." These Seven Rays are the first great modifications of matter or light, the two being interchangeable as Einstein's laws of conservation suggest.

White light is not the lack of color as one might assume, but is the totality of all colors within the visible spectrum. These various colors can be revealed through the use of a prism to refract or bend the light. The differing wave lengths (or frequencies) are effectively split away from each other by the shape of the prism. Water has a similar effect, producing a rainbow in the sky under the right weather conditions. In the same way the rays are contained in the unity of this force. Individually, they each form an aspect or quality of the synthesized whole. Combined they are once again unity. In a sense they are the seven notes in the scale of life. In the case of the rays, each is said to have all of the qualities present, but one predominant. If what I have been saying from the beginning is correct, and all that is manifested is alive with this single force, then these rays constitute *living entities* that combine in a greater organism. This is as we would expect based on Keys Five and Six. As it is above, so it is below, and we see the embracing of these differentiated living forces within the living unity.

In scripture they are referred to as "The Seven Lords (sometimes Lamps or Fires) Before the Throne." The Occult classics refer to the Seven Solar Logoi. As we have discussed, Logos is the Greek word for word; Logoi is the plural. This is the One Life, differentiated for the first time into component parts that will then influence all that is created. They are living conditions, for all is life. They are aspects of the One Life as we are aspects of it on another level. Each one of these great entities is manifesting through an entire Solar System. All are parts of a great Constellation that is the manifestation of "X."

Everything is alive and manifesting in accordance with its frequency and just as light broken down into its component frequencies appears as the differing colors of the spectrum, so each of these rays or Solar Logoi is associated with a color and a quality. Our sun is the Logos of the Second Ray, so in that respect the statement "God is Love" is true esoterically. Remember, we made up these names and in the greater scheme of things they are meaningless labels. Having said that, I will list them here and then we can examine them in expression in various ways.

They are:

Ray One – Will or Power
Ray Two – Love/Wisdom
Ray Three – Intelligent Activity
Ray Four - Harmony Beauty and Art
Ray Five – Concrete Mind and Science
Ray Six – Devotion
Ray Seven – Ceremonial Magic and Order

The Rays in Humanity

Let's take a look at how these different qualities work out in expression through the human consciousness. Each of us is essentially a Soul expressing itself through a personality and through the Law of Resonance, one of these aspects of the One Life which overshadows all forms of activity will dominate in that area of human expression. We refer to this as the Soul Ray. Due to my Soul Ray, I will have certain affinities based on frequency and quality, which will govern my activity; in this case Soul expression. The same holds true for the personality. One of these qualities that we are going to discuss will *color* the activity of my personality expression as a whole. The personality is also a triplicity, as we discussed in Chapter 6 on the anatomy of consciousness. There are the Physio-etheric, Astral, and Manasic Bodies, and each of these is also governed in its expression by one of these rays. Even the Soul is an expression of a spiritual essence, and we have called the individualized spark of that cosmic flame the Monad, so there is obviously going to be a vibratory frequency involved and as always, resonance and affinity must govern, so there is a monadic ray association.

We will not focus on the Monadic Ray because in most of us, really all of humanity, it is not a dominant force of expression. Some of us are beginning to live as Souls in the world but monadic consciousness lies far ahead. The Personality Ray does not even govern expression or become clearly evident until a certain amount of integration is achieved. This lack of integration literally means that the three bodies are still running around as individuals fighting for control rather than working together in any meaningful way. My head says this, my gut wants that, and my body ends up doing whatever the winner of this internal tug of war dictates.

In the case of the personality we need to consider the ray of the mind or mental body which will govern the person's mental approach to life, or what could be called the path of least resistance when dealing with mental issues. This will give us an idea of how her mind works. Then we must consider the ray of the emotional body, which will govern the emotional life of the person in question. What tugs the heartstrings of this individual? Of course there must be an associated ray for the physical body as well. Even physical matter is actually energy and all energy vibrates, has a frequency, and affinities that correspond all the way up to these 7 primary divisions of that energy. Essentially we have five rays to concern ourselves with, in regard to the human being and the one additional for the Monad, which for the most part, other than stating that it is always one of the first three of the trinity itself there is not much we can say. So we will look at the rays of:

The Soul
The Personality
The Mental Body
The Emotional Body
The Physio-Etheric Body

As we examine these qualities, it is important to note that more than one body can be governed by the same ray. When we are dealing with the Soul Ray we are dealing with that aspect of our being that motivates us into activity. It is the *why* of the incarnation. What is the Soul's purpose for entering into the lower worlds of human affairs?

The personality represents the medium through which this purpose is brought to bear; the *how* of expression or more clearly the nature of the vehicle of the Soul. It's time we take a look at these seven qualities and then see how they might interact with each other on various levels of human expression. In each case we will see the quality, a color associated with it and the areas of activity where its influence is felt in the individual as well as the group.

The Aspects

The First Ray – Will – Purpose – Power – Governmental Activity

Its color is seen in two ways. In its synthetic nature and as the totality of the others it is seen as white. Once differentiated, in its relationship to the others it is seen as red. It is the driving force in manifestation. It drives evolution, and aspiration. It is the ray of government and government is an expression of the will of the people governed. We discussed these ideas in more detail in Chapter 10 on the Trinity.

The Second Ray – Love/Wisdom – Soul – Consciousness

Its color is indigo blue. It is the cohesive force in nature - The power of attraction in expression in the Mineral Kingdom as gravity, and the higher kingdoms as Love. It is that which tends to assimilate, draw together and synthesize into one harmonious whole, any condition in the universe. So, if you have a Second Ray Soul, you will tend to try to bring things or people together. You will tend toward inclusivity. It governs Educational systems. It is the teaching ray and the ray of the philosopher, and the esotericist.

The Third Ray – Intelligent Activity/Adaptability

It governs Nature and its color is green. It is also expressed in finance and culture. It really governs the manifestation of physical matter and is sometimes called the ray of active intelligent matter or universal mind. Mind is an organizing force. It expresses itself in the organized growth of crystals in the Mineral Kingdom, and through every conceivable level of intelligence. This carries up to and presumably well beyond the arrogant little human mind. It also represents a synthesis in a way, because it manifests in four subsidiary rays that we refer to as the four *Attributes of Divinity*. You will see that each in its own way is an expression of a form of intelligence and activity.

The Attributes

The Fourth Ray – Harmony Beauty and Art

It is sometimes referred to as the ray of "harmony through conflict" and its color is yellow. This ray colors all creative expression, art, and music. It is the ray of the human family collectively (the fourth Kingdom). It is interesting to note that the Fifth Ray governs the Animal Kingdom, the Sixth Ray governs the Plant Kingdom, and the Seventh Ray governs the Mineral Kingdom. As you can see, creation is a vast web of interrelated energies of varying types and qualities, based on vibratory frequency, manifesting on varied planes of density.

The Fifth Ray – Concrete (lower) Mind – Science – Analytical Thought

This energy governs the scientist and his activity, as well as technology of any sort. It is the ray of mind for many of us. Its color is orange and it is showing its dominance in the culture of the West. We are said to be the fifth sub race of the fifth root race of our system.[50] In this context I am not speaking of Americans, or white people, or for that matter bald smart people with glasses. Remember the Esotericist sees man as a conscious entity, not the body that this entity has chosen to create as

---

[50]   This is dealt with at length in The Secret Doctrine and the collective works of Alice A. Bailey. There will be seven root races, each with seven sub-races in our planetary system.

a vehicle. There is no time in this work to get into a deep discussion of the progression of the races but I thought the double association with the Fifth Ray was worth mentioning. It also illustrates another type of relationship to this intricate picture of creation.

The Sixth Ray – Abstract Idealism - Emotionalism and Devotion

It is seen in dedication and especially in Religious expression. Its color is a silvery rose, although sometimes it is characterized as a light blue as well. This ray is particularly important in the effect it has had on humanity throughout the Piscean Age. We have seen two millennia of fundamental devotion to emotionally charged systems of faith, which have tended to pull away from each other in an effort to assert exclusivity. The Sixth Ray's influence is beginning to wane and in its place we see the waxing of another force, ushering in the Aquarian Age, that of the Seventh Ray. It is important to note that what we characterize as desire has a mental aspect to it. There is a thought process involved in what we *want*.

The Seventh Ray – Ceremonial Magic – Law and Order – Organization

Its color is violet, and it is a healing energy. The violet devas are the builders of our etheric doubles.[51] As this influence grows and the idealism of the Sixth Ray fades, we see conflict in the world. It is a result of these influences, the passing of an age and the re-focusing of energy in a different direction. The coming "New World Order" which is spoken of by some with fear is real but it is not a threat because this new order cannot be inflicted or forced. Further, it will not bring about cooperation and peace because it will be the result of those things. As we have seen, for the physical world to change consciousness must change first. You cannot have a realization for someone else. We all must come to conscious conclusions on our own and then use that new perspective in governing our interactions with each other.

---

[51]   Alice A. Bailey - *A Treatise on Cosmic Fire* (New York: Lucis Publishing Company 1925)

The inquiry into your ray makeup can be an intriguing and enlightening part of the process of self-discovery. You may change your mind many times or feel perfectly comfortable with your initial ray hypothesis. We are all different and yet we are all the same. Let's look at what I have been able to come up with in regard to myself as an example. All of you will at one time or another begin to ponder what your rays are, if you have not already begun this lifelong experimental investigation. Incidentally, the two books by Alice Bailey entitled Discipleship in the New Age I and II,[52] are an invaluable tool in the inquiry into ones ray makeup. The Master Djwahl Kuhl's letters to individual Disciples are given, detailing their strengths and struggles, as well as their ray types. This allows you to look at the psychological makeup of a Disciple similar to yourself and use the ray descriptions as a template to help you discern your own. I have not had my rays read or given to me. This is something only a Master can truly do. Like anything else it falls to the individual to find his way.

Soul – Second Ray – I am inclusive, philosophical in my nature and I have been told I am a natural teacher, which is something that makes me very happy to hear. It's important to me and in every given situation throughout my life, from martial arts to the corporate world, I have enjoyed and found ways to train and teach people. For me this seems an unavoidable choice, and it brings me great joy. Many who have a Sixth Ray Soul may think they are on the Second Ray because they are very loving, but all Souls are love and you may be looking at that very devotional part of yourself.

Personality – A bit tougher. I have a lot of will that drives me forward so I see the possibility of a first ray personality but there is also an aspect of me that is always trying to moderate situations. Whenever someone comes to me in conflict I tend to try to offer a softer interpretation of what is going on; seeing from the other side what might have been the motivating factor in some behavior being described. I am also a lifetime

---

[52] Alice A. Bailey – *Discipleship in the New Age: Volume I* (New York: Lucis Publishing Company 1944) and Alice A. Bailey - *Discipleship in the New Age: Volume II* (New York: Lucis Publishing Company 1955)

musician, a multi-instrumentalist, singer/songwriter, and a recording engineer. Music characterizes and permeates my life, so there is a lot of Fourth Ray energy there as well. I do believe for these reasons I have a Fourth Ray personality, but the jury isn't back yet.

Mind - I have a very analytical mind and that leads me initially to the Fifth Ray. I want to take everything apart and see how it works. Sometimes, I can even put things back together. I want to see how everything fits. I have made much my living as an engineer. This doesn't mean I'm smart, and being smart would not mean you had a Fifth Ray mental body. If you were very dedicated to learning and studious in your mental approach it might be an indication of a Sixth Ray mental body. In a three day immersion seminar on the subject I was asked by one of the facilitators to consider the idea that my mind is actually resonant with the Third Ray, because I am interested in and understand abstract concepts, like those found in quantum mechanics. These principles sometimes defy logic, at least human logic. So here again, I am in a process of knowing, rather than being in possession of a crystalized thought.

Emotional – I am very devoted in my approach to emotional areas of my life. I am a very dedicated student, husband and father, so there is a real possibility that I have a Sixth Ray emotional nature. I have in the past been very prone to anger, which is the down side of this kind of affinity. I am very idealistic and when I was younger and less in control of my emotions I felt a significant amount of righteous indignation. All of these are indications of a Sixth Ray Astral Body. I believe my more recent ability to stay steady in spite of these idealistic tendencies, represents a move toward Soul life and focus, rather than the more rare but possible migration from one ray to another.

Physical – Here I feel I am First Ray. I am small in stature but very physically driven. I can carry half my body weight on my back into the mountains. The last thousand feet of a climb up a peak can be a shear act of will, especially if you are not feeling well. I have never failed in an ascent because I just could not imagine not finishing. I mentioned music earlier but not the fact that my primary instrument is the drums.

If you have ever seen a rock drummer play it is very physical, so you can see where the artistic (Fourth Ray) personality finds a powerfully physical (First Ray) way of expressing this artistic energy, all with the loving sharing energy of the Second Ray Soul. I literally teach with my music because I am very conscious of what I write and put in front of people. My music is about life lessons and I hope to put into words things others struggle with in their own lives. As we continue this search we see how we can work in accordance with our rays instead of fighting them. It's like Tai Chi; using the tides of our lives for the momentum they provide instead of always swimming upstream or bucking the system, so to speak.

Below I have listed a number of Ray associations for various nations as they were enumerated in Alice Bailey's book *The Destiny of the Nations*.[53] I leave the validity to discretion of the reader, as does Ms. Bailey. I believe if you think about the history and culture of each nation in relation to these associations you will at the very least find it an interesting exercise.

Germany – The Fourth Ray governs the German nation's Ego or Soul. Its Personality Ray is the First Ray of government and power. So this purpose of harmony through conflict expresses itself through the arm of government.

Italy – Sixth Ray Soul (devotion) motivating their Fourth Ray Personality (beauty or art), so we see devotion expressed through art in the form of the magnificent religious art work of that nation.

USA – Second Ray Soul (synthesis) leads us to be a melting pot of all other cultures. With a Sixth Ray Personality, we are idealists and this has gotten us into trouble. We need to move from this sense of idealism that wants everyone to be just like us, to the Soul expression of love that allows everyone to be what they are.

---

[53]   Alice A. Bailey – *The Destiny of the Nations* (New York: Lucis Publishing Company 1949)

CHAPTER 12

The Rays, The Logoi And The Hierarchy

Scripture has a very poetic way of describing things and the many layers of meaning I find as I read and learn the language of symbols intrigue me. We are at a point where we will focus on the importance of the Seventh Key to the understanding of this Ageless Wisdom. As with the closely related study of the Seven Rays, we will be investigating on a very esoteric level. The Gospel of John opens, "In the beginning was the word and the word was with God, and God was the word." It is an expression of "Will of God," the first aspect. Logos not only means word, it represents manifestation through sound or more importantly, vibration. Nothing is created prior to this vibration and it is organized by mind. We explored this as expressed in Genesis where, before separating the light from the darkness God spoke the words "Let there be light." The thought is expressed as sound or vibration and is a statement of intent, which is followed immediately by the response of the universal pre-existent pre-matter (mulaprakriti) and a change occurs. In this case it is the very first change, and represents The One divided into two. As Lao Tzu stated, "From the two comes the three, and from the three all things come."

In this first act of creation we have seven words of power emanating from the One Life, God, X, or He about whom naught can be said, manifesting as the Seven Solar Logoi or Seven Lords Before the Throne.

A form of differentiated consciousness is now emanating from "The One" in accordance with the laws of the universe.

Our sun, the Second Ray Logos, is part of a great constellation. As we have said, every one of the Logoi manifests all seven of the rays, with one predominant in its nature. The sun manifests this energy through the seven sacred planets of our Solar system via the Planetary Logoi, repeating the creative process with seven rays of energy issuing forth from him. The overriding influence of the Second Ray will color expression throughout the entirety of his system. Each one of these great entities is manifesting through a solar system and in turn each of them repeats the process through the emergence of the Planetary Logoi.

You may assume because we are here on earth, that it is one of the seven sacred planets within our solar system. There is certainly a lot going on here and with only nine planets traditionally, and now that we are down to eight according to science (after Pluto's downgrading to a dwarf planet) our odds seem really good. It's just not the case. If it makes you feel any better, the Esoteric Sciences acknowledge twelve planets, so Pluto is back in but the definitions are different and the Earth does not make the short list anyway. One of the things the evolution of the human race provides is the redemption of matter through its contact with our consciousness. Our redemption will bring the redemption of the earth as well. We are all connected.

These seven great consciousnesses manifest through twelve planets, so if this is true, it is obvious that some of the Logoi are manifesting through more than one. The seven sacred planets are: The Sun, Saturn, Jupiter, Mars, Venus, Mercury, and the Moon. The moon does not fit the definition of a planetary body scientifically because it orbits a planet and not a star and the sun doesn't because it is a star. Remember, the definitions are different and we are not talking about the manifestation or form anyway, we are talking about the underlying living energy that is the source of the manifestation.

The Soul of the Earth's Planetary Logos relates to a great being known as Sanat Kumara in the way your Soul relates to your personality in physical plane expression. He is the being that is referred to in the book of Daniel as "The Ancient of Days" and in manifestation he is the sum total of life on our planet. His is the great body in which we physically function as cells. According to the Book of Acts, "He in whom we live, move and have our being." (Acts 17:28)

18 million years ago Sanat Kumara came to earth with a hierarchy of beings to form the first spiritual government here. Animal man showed the capability of becoming human and so this group was to serve as guides of the race. In a sense, the individuation of humanity coincides with the realization of self-consciousness for the planet as a whole. As you would expect, this new guidance for a fledgling race comes in the form of seven areas of creative activity, governed by those first great divisions of spiritual expression, The Seven Rays.

Let's look at it next to our government so we get an idea of how some of these relationships work. The use of thought experiments helps physicists to bring mathematical abstractions into perspective and this is a technique that should help us clarify the idea of a Hierarchy. As long as we acknowledge the distortion created by fleshing out the indefinable, we may gain in understanding without getting caught in a dogmatic assertion.

Imagine Sanat Kumara as the President. In his cabinet, he has six advisers. They are referred to as the six "Kumaras" or "Buddha's of Activity." These are the inhabitants, for lack of a better word, of Shamballa.

Working within a deliberative body such as our Congress, there are seven major committees, each with a chairman or department head. The numbers assigned correspond to the Seven Rays. Each of these entities is the literal head of the Ashram of the particular Ray.

This is the only time I will deal with the Masters and their names because for some this idea is difficult to accept. This is in part because of the personification of these entities and the association with their earthly personalities. It's back to the "old man on a cloud" image and I don't believe it's helpful. People tend to get caught up in learning about teachers like The Christ rather than paying attention to their teachings. Remember, they are masters of wisdom and masters of themselves. The purpose of self-discovery is to master yourself, not to dominate others. As you read these descriptions, note the ray association with the responsibility of each particular Ashram and its head.

The Hierarchy

The Manu: Will and Government - The Will or Power of God. In every case you will easily see the Ray Association governing the area of responsibility and the activity of the Ashram.

The Boddhisatva: Love/Wisdom - He is known as Lord Maitreya, The Christ (who overshadowed Jesus), The Imam Madhi, or Krishna. This is the Second Ray of Love/Wisdom and it is the education department. Maitreya/Christ is the world teacher; the teacher of the Angels and the Masters alike. He is the head of the hierarchy.

The Maha Chohan: Active Intelligence - He is known as "The Lord of Civilization" and is responsible for the governing of cultural expression. This department breaks into four sub departments as the Third Ray or Aspect of Divinity has expression through the four subsidiary attributes.

The Master Serapis: Harmony Beauty and Art, as discussed.

The Master Hilarion: Concrete Mind - He appeared before humanity as Saul of Tarsus who was later transformed into St. Paul when he was "blinded by the light" for three days after his experience on the road to Damascus. He also came before us in the personage of Martin Luther to help reform Christianity.

The Master Jesus: Devotion and Religious Expression - He was the vehicle of Maitreya, and in this incarnation he went through the initiatory process with Maitreya. He is now a Master as well, after having undergone that process. He was previously incarnated as Joshua of Nun who felled the walls of Jericho, and got God to stop the sun and moon so he could keep fighting. He was at that time, a Third Initiate. His incarnation as Jesus was dedicated to taking the fourth and fifth Initiations as Christ/Maitreya took the sixth and seventh. His life was characterized by sacrifice up to and including the crucifixion.

In my heart I believe that his ultimate sacrifice was willingly allowing the overshadowing of Maitreya at the River Jordan. In a sense he was watching his own life from the perspective of an interested observer as it was directed by Maitreya (the overshadowing Soul). My father's last book *The Christ Epoch*[54] is the most complete work I have ever found on this process, and well worth reading for any student of religious science and symbolism. This great Soul later incarnated as Apollonius of Tiana. He healed again, walked on water again, raised the dead again, and they killed him again. They thought he was an antichrist, but according to occult philosophy he was the very same entity.

The Master Rakoczi: Cerimonial Magic and Order - He is also known as the Comte de St. Germaine. He was canonized by the church after making a two million dollar donation. His purpose was to use this new station to position himself as a liaison in a time of war and is purported to have used his influence to avoid much suffering and bloodshed.

Not all the Masters work with Humanity, but there are a few more who have been very involved in our development and you will come across their names as you study. The Master Morea, working on the First Ray with the Manu, as well as Koot Humi and Djwahl Kuhl (The Tibetan) known for their work on the Second Ray with Maitreya. These three are also the collaborators who aided Madame Blavatsky in her work on The Secret Doctrine.

In 1919 Djwahl Kuhl began to communicate and collaborate with Alice A. Bailey in the production of 24 books over the course of 30 years.

---

[54]   Anthony J Fisichella – *One Solitary Life – Book III: The Christ Epoch* (USA: Authorhouse 2008)

Alice Bailey claims authorship of only 4 of the books that bear her name. This incredible body of work took the teachings and organized them in a way that is favorable to the Western mind and is my most valued source and resource.

The Inner conclave of a Master's students is known as an Ashram and is composed completely of Accepted Disciples and Initiates. They gather in their Astral Bodies while the physical form sleeps. This characteristically happens between 10:00 pm and 5:00 am.

I would just like to take a moment as we close this chapter to reiterate some ideas about the Masters as I understand them. The Masters don't make claims and they do not demand obedience. They cannot work with those who need to be ordered around, and that is not a system which develops leaders who can be trusted with greater responsibilities over time. They don't need big houses, gifts and money. The Master owns everything but takes nothing. "Seek ye first the kingdom of God and his justice and all else will be rendered unto you." (Mathew 6:33)

They suggest a course of action. If you believe you are dealing with a Master you should not need to be coerced anyway. His suggestions are based on an understanding you don't have. It's like a parent who is properly guiding his kids. I had my son Ian convinced I could see the future because I knew what his life was going to look like, based on what I watched him doing. I am not magic. He was just not looking. You are looking out for your kids because they can't do it yet and only trust them with new tasks when they have shown responsibility in handling the ones they have. The last parallel is that when you do give them new responsibility it is not because they deserve a gift for *being good*. It is because they have shown themselves to be more useful and ready to make a greater contribution to the workings of the family. The Master is busy serving humanity. If you are interested in attracting the attention of a Master, then serve humanity, don't try to find and serve him. He is not interested in being revered but if you make yourself useful by expanding your consciousness and stabilizing your personality, he may enlist you in his work.

CHAPTER 13

The Seven Planes

We have looked at various aspects of consciousness and the creative process. We have discussed the energetic influences and the effects of vibration on the universe. Now we are ready to begin to tie all of these various pieces together in a deeper way, through the study of the Seven Planes of Manifestation. There are several ways to view the planes and my hope is to help you to understand not only their individual characteristics but also the relationships between them. This is a fascinating subject and really represents the field of play within which the process of conscious evolution we have been discussing takes place. Although, like all else in the universe, the planes must be at least provisionally considered as living energy. I will have to use certain allegories or parallels but it is important not to get stuck in any of them because I will be painting a picture of something I cannot describe directly. Over and over again we see the reason for the Seventh Key and the use of symbolism when referring to matters of higher thought, and our approach to our divine nature.

This will be an attempt on my part to point at it from a number of different directions using necessarily imperfect metaphors. This is really where all of the principles we have been discussing are woven together into the fabric of the universe, and my hope is that it will be the point where you will reach a useful understanding of the creative process. We have touched on the planes as a part of some of our other topics but we will now take an in depth look at how all of the pieces fit together. The first and most important thing I have to clarify is that these planes, although they are often pictured as one above the other, are more appropriately termed as existing within each other. The so called "higher planes" are better termed the "inner planes" as we will see.

The planes can first of all be seen as octaves of energy. This is the best metaphor I have to show how they are built upon one another rather than the two dimensional layer cake model we will reluctantly employ later. In standard musical notation, an octave is a series of notes which starts from any root note and contains all of the notes of its particular scale, up to and including the next occurrence of the root note itself. This is in a sense the eighth note and thus called the octave. The octave note is also known as the first harmonic and if we examine the frequency of the note we find that is always twice the rate of vibration. In America we tend to use a musical system based on a specific "A" note being 440 Hertz (denoted Hz) or cycles per second. The octave or next "A" will be measured at exactly 880 Hz. Interestingly, in the next octave it is again doubled to 1760 Hz, so the difference in raw frequency is much greater but what is of moment is the relationship between the two. This harmonic doubling is our first indication of these relationships and the idea that these notes reside within each other.

Musical instruments sound differently for many reasons but if a single note is observed on a spectrum analyzer, which shows (vertical) spikes representing volume along the horizontal line representing the audible frequency range, it will show that there is a marked difference in the levels of the harmonics and their strengths from one instrument to the next. Each A contains many A's and the strengths of those harmonics are affected by the resonance of the instrument, the nature of its construction, and the types of materials used. The construction will affect other aspects of the sound such as attack, sustain, decay, and fall off, which give other characteristics such as a percussive punch, but what we are concerned with here is the rate of vibration that gives the note its pitch.

On a string instrument like a guitar, if we pluck the string it begins to vibrate at a frequency which will be determined by its length, its composition (steel or nylon) and the tension it holds between the two stationary points which define its length. It will then seem to divide itself in half and the vibration will begin to form a figure 8. This doubling brings out that first harmonic detected in the spectrum analyzer. It doubles again and again and these harmonics will vary in strength based on those characteristics of the string's composition and the ability of the instrument to resonate at higher and higher frequencies. An acoustic guitar will sound brighter with metal strings than nylon ones. It will sound different with phosphor/bronze strings than with standard 80/20 bronze strings. The phosphor component allows the strings to bring out these higher harmonics more effectively without any change to the construction of the instrument because they are made of a harder, denser alloy.

In our analogy the planes represent octaves of energy, each at harmonic intervals which are resonant with similar intervals on other planes. The sub-planes are represented by the individual notes in the scale. The first sub-plane of each has a similar relationship to the first sub-plane of all of the others. Just as the notes in the octave, they interact across the planes because of this relationship. If I play that A on a piano all of the other strings tuned to that note will vibrate and this is one of the reasons the sound of a piano is so full. The interaction of the vibrations causes overtones not present in the original notes. These planes interact at ever finer levels and are figuratively the fabric of the universe from which all of creation is woven, as the interactions of all these varying energies bring about the manifested universe.

The Golden Mean[55] is another mathematical relationship that we see repeated over and over in nature. Both of these ideas support the repeating patterns we see as relationships between the differing planes.

---

[55] This ratio is approximately 1 / 1.618. In this ratio the relationship of the smaller number to the larger is the same as the relationship of the larger to their sum. It is easy to see how this pattern will repeat in ever increasing scale. It is also represented in the series of numbers known as the Fibonacci Numbers

The same building blocks, assembled in repeating patterns, according to natural law.

Another way to look at the planes is to describe them as dimensions. Not in the classic sense of height, width and depth but as varied levels of existence one within another. We don't have to look up to see heaven or the spiritual realm. Just as in the case of the Rays, they are refractions of the life force of the Logos that brought them into existence, based on an idea. They are still "of the one essence" but they are variances of that energy based on variance in frequency.

We can look at these planes as degrees of density as well. All of the notes played within a symphony share the environment which resonates to their sounds, based on the density of the air and the size and shape of the room. The atmosphere is able to resonate at the frequencies in the audible spectrum, which is why we have sound. The room or chamber acts as a reflector and causes vibrations to reverberate. This is a detectable effect of any change in the field of play. Change to a denser environment like water and sound can still travel but the efficiency and thus, tone will be affected.

Examination of the water itself reveals that it is the result of the combination of two of our atmosphere's gases, hydrogen and oxygen. When combined the molecules move at a slower rate and form a denser medium that resonates with slower vibrations. This also shows how the denser and more substantial material is made up of the finer and more rarefied matter of the so-called inner or *higher* planes. If we go even denser by removing (heat) energy we have the crystallization of the water into ice, which can either be an effective barrier to those same vibrations, or actually conduct them more efficiently if they are introduced into the medium in a different way. Of course, we have already discussed how some of these analogies can point us in the right direction, but can tend to break down if pushed too far.

The Solar Logos is the deity of our solar system, and we live and move and have our being within "His" body in a Spiritual sense. The earth is a living breathing organism and we live within her body in a physical, and yet Spiritual sense as well. Note how natural it is to associate the male and female principles to spirit and matter respectively.

There are seven major divisions of this refracted energy, and just as we discussed the refraction of white light to break it out into its component colors, we can imagine these dimensions as one within the other and yet always unified in the whole. Quantum Mechanics talks of the field, a field of quanta. Infinitesimal indivisible units of energy within which and from which all matter is created. Madame Blavatsky tells us matter, in its myriad forms, is "the totality of existence in the cosmos which falls within any of the possible planes of perception." As fine and rarified as the material becomes it is all material, although most of it evades our perception.

The lower and slower we go, the denser the substance. This is because heat is chemically defined as motion and the energy is low. If we add energy, we add movement, and the density will decrease. You can melt iron by adding enough energy which gets the molecules moving faster and farther apart. It is still iron as a liquid, and will return to its solid state when it has radiated away the excess energy and as a consequence, slowed its vibration.

Everything vibrates, and consciousness can be defined as sensitivity to certain ranges of frequency with the various tools at its disposal, and the mind as the interpreter. We can't see all light but we can see a range of it. Visible light is a frequency range of electromagnetic radiation that is detectable by the human eye. The only thing that separates what your microwave uses to cook, the waves your radio picks up and visible light, is frequency. The same can be said of red light and blue light. They vary from each other in frequency alone. The blades of a fan seem to disappear when they move out of the range of our mechanism's ability to detect them, as the motor increases speed. You get the illusion (because of the time it takes to process the information) that you are seeing right through the blades. They appear to shade the area behind them because a certain amount of the light is being blocked. This processing time is why the series of still pictures in a movie or video appear as smooth movement. It is all perception. Each of the planes is a range of vibration that can be subdivided and we will be subdividing them. It should be noted that other systems exist that divide the vibrations in the manifested universe in different ways. This is by no means the only way to define the creative process or environment but I find it a very useful set of guidelines.

Another, if perhaps less intuitive way of looking at these planes is that they can be seen as a form of consciousness. All is life, and part of the unified substance of the universe. If that pushes the limits of your religious or pragmatic belief system, ask yourself those same two questions. What lies outside of God? For most the answer is "nothing." Then ask "what part of God is not alive?"

My physical body is my mechanism in the physical world. My astral body is made up of astral matter and resides on the Astral Plane. This represents a higher octave of energy in relation to the physical planes but lower than that of mind. Each plane is built upon the ones that precede it, from the finest matter outward to the densest. In this way you can see how the physical world is seen esoterically as a product of the mind. Energy follows thought. We will get deeper into that as we proceed.

As I said early on, these planes do NOT reside above one another but they are often pictured that way because of the limitations of a two dimensional graph. (See Figure 1) It is an effective way of looking at them if you don't allow yourself to get stuck in a literal interpretation. Hopefully the analogies used above will defend us against that logical slip.

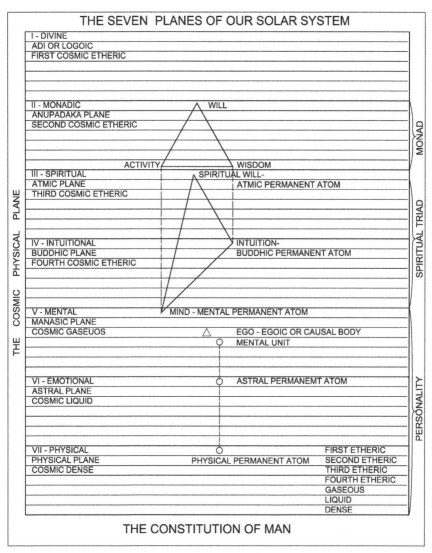

THE SEVEN PLANES OF OUR SOLAR SYSTEM

I - DIVINE	
ADI OR LOGOIC	
FIRST COSMIC ETHERIC	

II - MONADIC — WILL
ANUPADAKA PLANE
SECOND COSMIC ETHERIC

ACTIVITY — WISDOM

III - SPIRITUAL — SPIRITUAL WILL-
ATMIC PLANE — ATMIC PERMANENT ATOM
THIRD COSMIC ETHERIC

IV - INTUITIONAL — INTUITION-
BUDDHIC PLANE — BUDDHIC PERMANENT ATOM
FOURTH COSMIC ETHERIC

V - MENTAL — MIND - MENTAL PERMANENT ATOM
MANASIC PLANE
COSMIC GASEUOS — EGO - EGOIC OR CAUSAL BODY
— MENTAL UNIT

VI - EMOTIONAL — ASTRAL PERMANEMT ATOM
ASTRAL PLANE
COSMIC LIQUID

VII - PHYSICAL — FIRST ETHERIC
PHYSICAL PLANE — SECOND ETHERIC
COSMIC DENSE — PHYSICAL PERMANENT ATOM — THIRD ETHERIC
— FOURTH ETHERIC
— GASEOUS
— LIQUID
— DENSE

THE COSMIC PHYSICAL PLANE

MONAD

SPIRITUAL TRIAD

PERSONALITY

THE CONSTITUTION OF MAN

Personality - ego, animal soul
EGO - Human Soul
Spiritual Triad - Solar Angel, Divine Soul, Jivatma
Monad - Spirit

The Cosmic Physical Plane

There are seven of these dimensions in which the Logos or God of our system finds expression. This is His entire range of evolution, most of which is beyond our comprehension. This is why this great being is sometimes referred to as "He about whom naught can be said." To begin with, we will be looking at the seventh or Physical Plane within his range of consciousness, which actually makes up the entirety of our range of manifested expression. As you will see this is complex enough on its own. We will come back to the rest of the Cosmic Planes later. Once we have looked into our realm of existence, we will be in a better position to apply the Law of Correspondences to project our understanding into these un-knowable areas of the manifested universe, at least on a theoretical level.

The Cosmic Physical Plane is divided into seven sub-planes that constitute *our* total range of evolution and expression. I am going to give you three different sets of names for them because you will run into them in your studies. The first two sets of names include the Sanskrit terms and the approximate English translations.

Keep in mind as we proceed that the top two are the planes of divine manifestation or expression. This is where God consciousness (a finite God, if that makes sense) evolves and unfolds itself. The next five are where we evolve as lower expressions of that divine consciousness. Of these, the bottom three are the worlds of the evolution of the personality. These are the fields of experience for the human Soul to unfold and express its power so that it is no longer just potential. As we raise our consciousness to higher levels we find ourselves where the initiate is evolving himself. Having transcended personality expression through discipline and harmlessness, he is being initiated into monadic consciousness and Mastery. The guides of the race are still evolving as well.

From the finest to the densest they are as follows:

Adi – The Divine Plane
Anupadaka – The Monadic Plane
Atmic – Self
Buddhic - Intuitional
Manasic - Mental
Astral - Emotional
Pranic - Physical

Our consciousness and consequently our field of evolution resides within the seventh or physical plane of the Logos. Even in its most rarified and spiritual level of expression, our reality is really a physical condition to this unimaginably high level of consciousness. Now, that sounds counter intuitive to most people. How is it that the subtleties of our world are beyond the sense and scope of a higher level of consciousness? Think for a moment about the world of an insect, like an ant. We can't possibly imagine what the world looks like to an intellect that small. We can imagine sand as boulders but that is a human interpretation of being small in comparison to the sand particles. What is the perception of the sand in the mind of "ant?" Incidentally, no matter how "high" our level of consciousness is in relation to that of the ant, we cannot communicate in any real way with the ant. We can perhaps observe its behavior and change its environment in a way that will alter that behavior but the ant will not know. It will just respond to the changes in a way that is consistent with its level of awareness.

We know many things about the sub-atomic world now because of the research that has been done in the last one hundred years or so. They have now verified through experimentation what was once very cutting edge theory about quantum "reality." We can use the sophisticated instruments science now has at its disposal to measure and detect evidence of what we will never perceive directly with our level of mind. The atom is mostly empty space, and is a fluid and ever changing condition in constant motion. It trades off electrons with other atoms and interacts in a world we see as nothing more than solid matter. This solid state is analogous to what the sum total of our physical world is to the mind of the Logos.

Let's define these planes with a little more clarity and then we can begin to examine the interactions and the creative process.

Adi – The Divine Plane - God undifferentiated. It is the source of both sides of duality. God divided the light from the darkness and so pre-exists them both. All is reducible to this plane. Everything else is built upon it. This is the unified un-manifest all-consuming fire described by Moses. To me this is the quantum field and represents pure potential.

Anupadaka – The Monadic Plane – God or the One Life differentiated for the first time. The word Anupadaka translates to "parentless." This is seen as the first level of manifested existence in our Solar System. It is not the product of anything already existent in the way we understand existence. It is rather the product of pure potential. Remember, Monads could be seen as the sparks of the all-consuming flame. The Monad is perfect in essence, but not perfect in its expression of that essence. The Monad is that which moves in and out of manifestation and yet remains.

Atmic - Atma translates to Self or Soul. This is the first time this spiritual essence has taken an envelope of matter and clothed itself in what is known as the Atmic Sheath. We now have the Monad in manifestation; in time and space. The prefix Maha means great, so a Mahatma translates to Great Self or Great Soul. We are all Mahatmas on the path to the realization of this fact.

Buddhic – Buddhi is Intuition, or more accurately, higher intuition. I am not referring to the instinctive gut level response this word brings to mind in most people. It is sometimes called reflective consciousness because it reflects the truth in and of its own pure and (relatively) undistorted nature. It is the capacity to apprehend truth without the necessity of a reasoning process. This is a deep *knowing* that cannot be related to another person who does not *know*. This is why it is sometimes said that Spiritual truth must be grasped "a priori" or first hand. Anything less is relegated to the realm of belief or faith.

Manasic – This is the Mental Plane. It is the realm of mind in its varying levels of expression from the lower concrete and reasoning mind to the higher abstract, imaginative and creative functions. Remember, it is where "man" gets his name for the human is "the one who thinks." This simple misunderstanding of the term man has caused much of the trouble in so called "organized religion" because men were seen as the only ones capable of spiritual understanding. Given the symbolic representation of the principles involved we are all male on a spiritual level, and female or receptive of this spiritual energy on a material (or personality) level.

Astral – The Emotional or Desire Plane. Its name is really a misnomer because it is characterized more by mist and miasma than the clear starry sky. Emotions can fog the intellect, especially in the case of the lower emotions, like hate and fear. Higher ones like love and brotherhood tend us upward in our evolutionary journey.

Physical – The physical world we interact with every day and know with our various senses. We are going to use this as our model for the other planes for the obvious reason that we are most familiar with it, and can easily see the relationships between its seven sub-planes.

The Planes of Human Evolution

This part of our journey will take us from the bottom to the top (or outside, in). Merging back with the source is the goal of evolution in consciousness. Remember, consciousness is what truly evolves. Everything else is a reflection of that on some level. Involution brought us the physical world and now we are to consciously transcend it. Returning "whence we came and knowing the place for the very first time." (TS Elliott)

Before we proceed with that, I would like to introduce you to one more idea. Each plane unfolds what is known as a "principle." Webster tells us "Principle is the source and origin, that from which anything proceeds; the beginning, the first." So, the principle comes first and it is not the result of any particular manifested plane of existence but the cause. Let's define these principles up front so we can incorporate that into our discussion as we proceed. For our purposes we will deal with the three lower principles of human endeavor and the two with which the initiate works.

Physical – The physical plane embodies the principle of Prana – The Etheric double of the physical form is made up of this energetic matter. We covered this idea at some length in Chapter 6 on the anatomy of consciousness.

Astral – The principle unfolding on the Astral Plane is known as Kama. This roughly translates to the word Desire. The Kama Sutra is an exploration of the desire nature.

Mental - Manas is the principle of mind in its varying forms of expression. We speak in terms of the lower concrete reasoning mind and the higher form of expression as the abstract mind. This is the creative aspect of mind as an organizing force. The lower mind is limited to the recognition of the patterns set into place by the higher mind. Kama/ Manas or desire/mind is a term that reflects their close interaction. It is difficult to imagine a thought that does not produce an emotional response or an emotion that does not produce some kind of mental process. There are also the:

Buddhic – Buddhi – Higher intuition as earlier described.

Atmic – Atma – Self or Soul, but it is really the first expression of the self.

The Physical Planes

As with all of the planes, it is divided into seven sub-planes and while we can relate directly to them at least to a certain extent in the case of the physical, the same subdivisions are used for all of the planes of manifestation. Here is where the relationships really start to come to light.

The Solid Plane, or more accurately *sub-plane* – This is the lowest, slowest and densest type of matter in the universe. And yet we are told it is still energy; pure potential that has "collapsed" into form. It is the end product of the involutionary process and consequently the outer form we recognize.

Liquid – More malleable than the first in that while it is just as physical, the level of energy present raises the vibratory frequency and has the physical molecules bouncing off of each other at a greater rate, maintaining more space between them. Again we see how a different form is created by the same substance based on its vibratory frequency.

Gaseous – This represents more of the same. A greater level of energy producing higher vibrations and more space, creating a finer more malleable form of the very same substance as we discussed with the analogy of ice, water and steam. All matter exhibits these three states at different temperatures based on the density of the material and other factors. At very high temperatures even rock will melt and we have made a science of smelting liquid metal into various blends for specific purposes. Stars contain metals like magnesium in the gaseous state because of the incredible level of energy involved in what are really the smelting pots of the universe.

This is important because it extends beyond that simple analogy. I am solid to the touch but I am made predominantly of water. Water is a liquid, which in turn, is made up of two gases (hydrogen and oxygen). You can now see in the real world that the planes reside within one another and are made of the building blocks of the finer material expression. The outer appearance is a form created by the inner substance. Substance sub-stands or stands beneath the form. It is incorporated into the outer form. As above, so below.

Now if you refer back to Figure 1, we have four etheric sub-planes which are also within me and vitalize my physical structure. The gases that make up the liquid that is incorporated into the solid "me" are vitalized by an even finer substance that is really more energetic than it is material to our level of consciousness. All is energy and quantum physics tells us that energy is coalesced into material form by conscious observation, according to what is known as the Copenhagen interpretation of wave particle duality.[56] I disagree with this to a certain extent. I am not certain it is ever actually materialized, but simply perceived as material to the human state of consciousness, *by the human state of consciousness.*

Einstein once quipped in opposition to the Copenhagen Interpretation, asking if it had to be a human observer or "would a sidelong glance from a mouse suffice?" My answer is that if you are a human consciousness, it takes a human consciousness; if you are a mouse then a sidelong glance from *you* is enough to contribute to *your* perception of reality. This is how every consciousness is seen as creating its own reality, even though we are all living in a common environment. We all perceive it a little bit differently… as does the mouse. The closer we are in our level of awareness, the more we share in our ability to perceive. In this case the resultant world view will be similar enough for us to interact effectively. As we observed earlier, we cannot communicate with the ant, but we can communicate with a dog, because we share enough similar equipment and level of awareness. Incidentally, as we raise that level or range of conscious perception, some of these previously imperceptible

---

[56] Copenhagen was an interpretation by Niels Bohr, Werner Heisenberg and their associates in Copenhagen in the period between 1924 -27. It deals with the idea of potentiality and probability in that until a measurement is taken (conscious observation) a particle can behave as a wave and be "spread out" over an area with no specific position, a phenomena know as its wave function. The act of measurement of either its velocity or position (both cannot be known simultaneously; due to what is known as Heisenberg's uncertainty principle) causes the wave to "collapse" into one of the possibilities described by its wave function and materialize.

realms come within this newly expanded range. This is where we find the energy healer who can see etheric imbalances and help re-direct the flow of energy back into a healthy rhythm.

These more energetic sub-divisions or levels of the physical plane are known as the Etheric Planes and are enumerated, as we move up in vibration, as follows:

4th etheric or simply, etheric
3rd etheric – also known as super-etheric
2nd etheric – the subatomic
1st etheric – the atomic

At the highest or atomic level, we are not talking about the atom of science; but an indivisible particle. The name atom doesn't work for that cartoon atom from your science book anymore and it really doesn't work here either. The true atom of the physical world is still divisible but once divided we are dealing with astral matter. We have entered the Astral Plane. In a sense we have simply taken another step along the continuum away from the material and toward the energetic. This is why your emotions affect you physically. The physical world is built upon the astral. It is all the same "stuff" just vibrating at higher and higher rates.

This may seem like a leap, but stick with me because it will all come together soon. Our solid liquid and gaseous planes as well as the four etheric reside in the lowest sub-plane of what we are exploring, which if you remember, is the Cosmic Physical plane. I hope you are beginning to understand how the seven sub-planes of our physical world are on the solid sub-plane of the physical plane of the Logos and thus are perceived as solid matter. It is all dependent on the level and breadth of sensitive awareness, which is defined as a certain level of consciousness, and the vibratory frequencies it is able to detect. Consciousness is the ability to detect a range of vibratory frequencies and the consciousness of the Logos is tuned to an infinitely higher octave of frequencies than ours.

If we see the seven planes of human evolution as the seven sub-planes of Logoic Physical, and the total of our physical world in its seven subdivisions as the Solid sub-plane of the Logos, then the next set of planes (our Astral) would in their totality constitute the Cosmic Liquid Plane. The Astral Plane is in fact the Cosmic Liquid Plane as illustrated in the three names given for each plane on the left side of Figure 1. Remember the metaphors we use. In every case you can imagine, liquid is used to describe emotional states. The water of love is described as life giving sustenance to the emotional body. The desert is seen as lonely.

The Mental plane in its turn is the Cosmic Gaseous Plane. As we move up the scale we get to the true atom on the highest or atomic sub-plane of Adi. This is the true atom of the physical world and is far more subtle in its nature than the atom of science. It is the source of all manifestation in the system, and is that from which all of reality is built. This is mulaprakriti or pre-matter and it is also the quantum field from which all matter springs. Its first product is prakriti and from that, all of creation is brought into being, beginning with the Monadic Plane.

The Solar Angel

Upon the Monadic plane we find the Human Monad along with all of the other Monads. In the case of the Human Monad we are dealing with a spark of the divine flame that has become self-aware. This is the real you, and it is at one with the universe. It reflects the three aspects of divinity (Will Love and Activity) as we studied in the Trinity. This is the Monad in eternity. It is a fragment of the One Life and dwells in the eternal now.

One step below that, we begin to see its expression in time and space. It sends out a ray of energy down (or out) into the Atmic plane and on the highest sub-plane it appropriates an atom of the substance of that plane. Another extends into the atomic sub-plane of the Buddhic plane. A third Ray extends into the Manasic plane and joining them together we see the reflection of the Monad in time and space.

We have the manifestation of the Solar Angel (Atma-Buddhi-Manas) or; spiritual expression on the Atmic plane, loving Intuition on the Buddhic, and mental expression on the Manasic Plane. It has lost dimension in its decent in the same way that a reflection in a mirror is a distorted two dimensional representation of the three dimensional object. This "loss" is only apparent in its expression. Nothing is truly lost.

The Personality

The personality is your reflector. Everything in the universe is a reflection of the deity that creates it. It produces a mere impression of itself because of the degraded medium through which it is reflected. Man is made in God's image and is a reflection of that perfection in a less perfect environment. It is thus a less perfect expression.

From the Solar Angel downward we get the same principles of Will, Love and Activity reflected in the Causal Body and then again in the personality vehicles of the emotional, mental and physio-etheric bodies. This is that same force once again projected down into a denser medium and further distorted. Now you could say we are but a shadow of ourselves and no longer even a reflection. In the case of a shadow even the interior details and color of the image are lost and only the silhouette remains. This is still representative of some of the aspects of the original and changes as it changes, but we have come so far from the source that it is almost unrecognizable, with so much information lost.

The lower and higher aspects of the human consciousness meet on the mental plane. The highest expression of the personality is the concrete mind and is reflected on the lower Mental Planes. The lowest form of expression of the Solar Angel in the form of the abstract creative mind is reflected on the highest sub-plane of the Mental Plane. This is why the mind is seen as the gateway to Soul awareness. It is where our lower and higher aspects meet.

We must unify our lower and higher minds, and in order to do that we must meditate. In occult meditation we build the consciousness thread between the lower and higher mind, called the Antahkarana. We work with specific visualizations under guidance from those ahead of us on the path, so that when we are visualizing we are working in mental matter to construct this bridge of light. This is the channel through which the awareness of the true self is first glimpsed and the capacity for inspiration is contacted. We gain access to the raincloud of knowable things, as taught by Patanjali.

The process of unification starts in the personality. The integration of the mind and the physical body is mediated by the emotions or our desire nature. Desire starts the process and then is transmuted into Spiritual Will. Then we unify the personality with the Soul. The Disciple transcends the personality and is considered to be in the world, but not of the world. She is identified with the Soul and not the personality.

The Causal Body

On one of the upper three levels of the mental plane the Soul resides in what is known as the Causal Body. As we discussed, in The Old Testament it is spoken of as "The Temple of Solomon" or The Temple of the Spirit; built without hands or mortar or brick. It exists as an envelope of mental matter encompassing three permanent atoms from the lower planes. These are particles of this living energy from the highest (atomic) sub-plane of each of the lower three planes of personality unfoldment, the Physical, Emotional, and Mental planes. There it resides in between incarnations in what the Theosophical Society refers to as the "heaven world."

In order to incarnate, the Soul, in the manner of the Monad, sends out a ray of light/energy carrying these permanent atoms into the lower three worlds, constructing new vehicles with the quality it is capable of creating, based on past experiences and growth but without the memories contained in the physical form.

When we die we reverse the process of emanation described above and withdraw from the physical body into the astral world keeping the physical permanent atom intact. Without the support and coalescing force of the Soul, the physical body is dropped and decomposes, returning the physical matter incorporated in life, back to the living reservoir from which it was drawn. Ashes to ashes, dust to dust. As we discussed in Chapter 6 on the anatomy of consciousness, we withdraw after a time from the Astral Body as well, taking with us the astral permanent atom. The same happens with the Manasic Body and we now reside in the Causal Body in Devachan, until we incarnate again.

We have withdrawn all the qualities, capacities, and tendencies intact in the form of a vibratory signature on each of the planes of manifestation and retain those qualities as we assimilate the experiences and lessons learned on the lower planes during our "life." In this way we see that the Soul records not the experiences of each lifetime per se, but benefits from the growth experienced in the process.

The Logos

Let's take a look at how the Logos of our Solar System creates and see how that correlates to creation at the level of human consciousness. As above, so below. We can once again incorporate the symbolism of Genesis and see that this idea of creation has been taught to us over thousands of years. We have assigned the same names to the cosmic planes in the early part of our conversation and can now look with some clarity at the descriptions of this creative process, symbolized in the ancient texts.

The mind of God, residing on the Cosmic Mental Plane, conceives of a purpose he wants to see manifested. Note those words. At this point he has simply created a thought form; an idea. Nothing is created but the thought itself until it is infused with desire. The Astral Plane rests between the mental and physical worlds. The desire to see this thought come to fruition in a physical way galvanizes him into action within the sphere or ring-pass-not of his system. Remember, in accordance with our Sixth Key, he too lives within an even greater being.

The description of the first creation in Genesis is that the earth was null and void and that darkness was upon the face of the deep. We are not told how there could "be" anything prior to this, yet the spirit of God is said to have hovered above the waters before any creative act had been performed. Waters? Desire! The Cosmic Astral Plane is obviously the liquid plane of the higher level of consciousness within whom this Logos lives and moves and has his being. This is the liquid plane of "He about whom naught can be said." Then we have the first act, which is not the separation of the light from the darkness, but the spoken words "Let there be light." Vibratory rhythm symbolized by sound, resonates through the pre-existent medium (mulaprakriti, or the deep) of the universe, resulting in the organization of that medium into form. Creation is the result of conscious choice facilitated by the organizing force of mind and brought into physical reality through the power of desire.

Through this process, the mind of God, clothed in the love of God, brings into being the first (atomic) sub-plane of the cosmic physical plane, Adi. Our highest plane of existence now begins to subdivide through the types of relationships we discussed in the Trinity. The three becomes the seven. And then "all things come." (Lao Tsu) The projection of this spiritual force through the Monad to create a "reality" is like the projection of light through a holographic plate. A creation is manifested that will reflect the whole in every part because the Monad exists in unity.

CHAPTER 14

The Creative Process In Man

It has not been my intent in a work such as this to present an in depth esoteric study, although I know much of what I have said may take a while to sink in. My purpose has been to bring together some fairly complex ideas in a way that makes them simple to understand and above all else, useful. We have just undertaken an exploration of the creative process and the nature of the universe it has created and within which it continues to create. I find these things interesting and intriguing but the whole situation begs the question, how will understanding these things help the average person create for herself a better life?

As a reflection of the greater creative consciousness, we must reproduce the same process within our range of expression, in order to create in our world. We must think and create (or access) an idea. Then we must infuse it with desire and the force of our aspiration and act. Once we do this it must manifest. The system has no choice but to respond to the rhythm and pattern of our thought forms. Depending on how powerful the desire and how clear the thought form we are capable of creating, we all get varying results. Most of us are totally ineffective at doing this because we don't know we are doing it, or even that we can.

We feel like the victims of circumstance when our lives are not fulfilling but we are the victims of our own habitual thinking and programming.

We were programmed by our parents first and then by the school system and our friends. Our experiences have built up in us patterns of behavioral response that we don't even know are the reasons for the way we behave. What is known as Psychology has actually been fairly effective in working on these personality defects. Maybe it should be called "Personology" because it has nothing to do with the Psyche or Soul involved. It is a system of behavioral modification and so, is focused on personality response. Drugs are often used to curtail behaviors and set the personality on an even keel. A drug cannot affect the Soul. They affect us mentally, emotionally and physically because of the interaction with the physical body chemistry and can be helpful in some cases but the constant introduction of one chemical after another, with a pill for every ailment and another for the new ailment caused by the first pill has got to stop.

You already have the power to create your ideal life. As a culture, we have let those creative muscles go a bit soft because too few people know they have them. Desire is not enough and neither is thought, or action. We need all three and we need to have them moving in harmony with each other. The moment I start to think, I begin to stir the matter in the astral world, because it is composed of mental matter, which has slowed and coalesced on a lower plane.

Thoughts are said to precipitate downward. A thought will trigger memories associated with emotional states. A projection into the future creating fictitious circumstances can be even more powerful than actual physical world experience in creating fear or desire and this will immediately cause a change in a person's physiology as if the thought were an event *because it is*. It is just not a physical plane event, yet.

The thoughts I have about what *is happening physically* are the reasons for an emotional response in that situation as well. I only react with fear when I am aware of physical danger mentally. The squirrel doesn't know the car will crush it. It only knows the car is big and doesn't even know it knows that. Animals don't project off into the future and anticipate what may happen, so they don't feel the mental anguish we inflict on ourselves. They live much more completely in the moment like a toddler does, and as a result their joy as well as their sorrow are much more pure.

There is a positive side to this, in that we can tell ourselves that a particular sadness or pain will pass. If you have ever seen a child who has lost her balloon, as my daughter Shannon did on returning from Disneyland, you know there is no life without it. The end has come. She has no idea that her future holds many balloons and that she will soon forget this devastating event. The idea is to blend the ability to project into the future, and analyze the past, with a vigilant awareness of the present. Then you can focus on whatever is most effective and useful at any particular time.

You cannot create change physically. Nothing has ever been created without first being imagined. The imagination is the image making faculty of the mind. Every item in your room or in your entire life started out as an idea in the mind of some creator; the mountain came from the mind of God/Life and the peton and carabineer from the mind of a climber. You can't *fight for an idea* physically, or force someone to love you. This kind of thinking will fade as you understand these planes and how we function on each of them.

We are told in the Old Testament that Man is made in God's image. This does not mean God looks like a man. If we are stuck with that single image of God as an old man in the sky, or what my friend Eli calls an imaginary friend, then I am an atheist. Man is a consciousness, endowed with creative ability. That is certainly a possible description of God, if taken to a higher level. Man operates through the same principles and reflects them in a lower degree. He manifests in his seven planes and we manifest in our fraction of that reality.

The mind of God is operating in his mental world seven planes above ours, his heart on his Astral Plane reflecting a level of love we cannot imagine. The distance, if I can use such a word, between our reality and that of the Logos is immense, and yet we are both here together and made from each other.

We are the microcosm to *His* macrocosm. Look at how far we must go to reach the mind of God, but the gift of Humanity is the ability to push back the barriers of our awareness. We do this each day in little ways over the course of a lifetime. Fortunately, we have multitudes of lifetimes and eventually we will re-unite in consciousness with this creative force and know the place, this *state of being*, for the very first time. This is where the path leads and we are all travelling it together and all feeling alone as we do. That feeling of loneliness is an illusion caused by the unique way we each express the unity of the all, through our varied experience. It can be an enriching experience if only we observe, rather than being overcome by it.

The Seven Keys that I have used as a tool for framing this reality can be summed up as follows; **There is but one living force in the universe, pervading every form it creates, manifesting cyclically in a series of emergent wholes and parts, as a result of vibration, in order to evolve and perfect its awareness on every level of manifestation, the process on each level being a reflection of the original creative process on its own plane.**

In order to create, we must be a reflection of this universal process and we are, although we have become entwined in our individual dreams through our deep identification with them. We are not the dream as much as the dreamer and we can come to a place in awareness where we are in the world but not of it. We are the conscious observer and creator of the reality we live in each and every day. In order to take control of the creative process, we must take control of our thought process. Creativity as we know it takes place first on the Mental Plane. All is energy and energy follows thought. Observe what it is you think about most and you will know why you have created the world you know. If you can't identify what it is you are thinking about most, look around you, for you will know the tree by its fruit.

Thought form Creation

The movie *The Secret* gave a simple treatment of a complex idea involving this creative process and right now, I would like to give you a bit more of the story. We touched on this earlier with the idea of precipitation. A thought infused with desire causes action. The movie can lead you to believe that the desire is the only thing you need. I want something bad enough and it just shows up. One of the speakers talks about a house in a picture on his vision board who actually moved into the house five years after putting it there. I met the actress Lindsay Wagner a few years ago and she told a very similar story. She and her husband were shopping in an area she had loved since she had first gone through it. There was even a specific "dream home" she had seen and wondered about. When she walked into a particular place she realized it was the exact house she had seen years before. She had set her sights on it, filed it away and gotten to work. Now having become a success, she found herself standing in the living room of her dream from years before. She turned and told her husband *"we are living here… and I'll explain later."* It is amazing what the power behind a clear vision or visualization can be.

My favorite interview is the one with Jack Canfield. He tells the story of seeing the periodical *The Enquirer* in a gas station on the way to do a talk. He thought that if they did a story on him, everyone would know about his book and everyone would buy it. Right after his talk he was approached by a reporter from… wait for it... The Enquirer! Oh my God it works!!! Well, guess what? He didn't just wish for the Enquirer article. He first wrote a book, then he did a public speaking tour, then he saw the Enquirer on a news stand. His first (or at least prior) wish/thought was to write a book, and he wrote it. The mental state must precipitate down through the emotional state and survive and thrive, prompting action. The moment that he saw the paper on the rack and had his thought connection could be seen more as tuning in on what was happening, rather than the cause of the interview. The reporter was likely on her way to the talk when he saw the paper. The wheels were in motion. The cause was his cumulative pattern of decisions and actions along the way.

The laws of nature are at your service when you are at the service of humanity. If you are simply wishing for a Porsche because you want one and not doing anything for yourself or anyone else, you will be wishing for a long time. If your desire is to create wealth for your own selfish purposes you may succeed but you will probably be miserable. If you are overly materialistic, it is possible that nothing will make you happy. You will not find solace in food or money or anything else. You will end up thinking someday "Is this all there is?" I believe that is a key turning point for every human consciousness. The realization that despite all your efforts to do the things we are all supposed to do, you still feel unhappy and sort of empty and you have to figure out why. It is likely what set you on the path that led you to this book.

Humanity is awakening at a rapidly increasing rate. The stream is moving and you are being carried along. If you are paddling with the current you will awaken more quickly and if you are fighting it you will lag, but you are still being carried along. We are fast approaching a time when initiation will no longer be an individual event but that groups will be initiated en masse. The teaching is changing because humanity is changing and thus a new presentation of universal truth on a higher level is made available to mankind through our own efforts and, as Madame Blavatsky stated, "self-devised and self-induced methods."

There are seven additional keys you should know about and they have to do with this creative process and the art of self-actualization. They form the core of my next project. I will provide them here as seed thoughts for meditation or just food for thought.

The Seven Keys to Self Actualization

1. **All is Energy** - There is only One Life and this creative energy is reflected in all that we know as the universe. (Are you surprised?)
2. **Energy Follows Thought** - Mind is the organizing force of the universe. Energy is its source. Thus "Energy Follows Thought"
3. **Man is a Creator** - The human consciousness or Soul is a fragment of this spiritual essence and the creator of its own reality.
4. **The First creation of Man is his Lower Self** - This creative entity inhabits a multi-faceted organism it uses in order to experience and express itself on the physical emotional and mental planes.
5. **Consciousness affects the material from which its vehicles are created**.

6. **Thought + Desire = Action** - The Creative process requires a thought, infused with desire to create the action necessary to bring it to fruition on the physical plane.

7. **Discipline prepares the lower self for the influx of energy from the spiritual essence**. The gateway is opened through the proper use of meditation.

Live, Love, Learn, and Create.
'Till next we meet.

APPENDIX A

Progressive Relaxation Meditation

This exercise will not only give you a simple way of releasing tension and gaining full relaxation in your physical body, it will bring you into closer contact with it. You will learn to listen to it and control it and work in harmony with it, relaxing away tension in muscle groups you are not even aware of as you begin. You will become able to focus your consciousness in a specific area and ascertain what is going on there.

Sit comfortably finding a position that uses a minimum of effort to maintain. Keep your spine erect and neck straight or tilted very slightly forward. Some prefer to meditate cross legged but for this exercise it is actually better to sit in a chair with your feet flat on the floor and hands folded in a comfortable way on your lap or flat on your thighs.

After centering and relaxing your physical body, focus your attention on your toes. You may want to wiggle them for a moment to really feel them. What is the sensation you feel? Feel the pressure of the floor beneath them. Is it a carpet, or are they pressed against a hardwood floor? Allow all else to fade below the threshold of your consciousness and just experience the world through that small area of your body as you consciously relax those muscles.

Now include the entirety of your feet. Feel the pressure of the heels pressing into the floor and realize that you cannot actually relax your toes alone.

The muscles that control them are in the feet. Feel the relaxation of all of those muscles and the input from the sensing nerves in the skin. Are there any tense muscles in the arch of your foot? Try to let it go and then include your ankles and the muscles of your calves and shins. There can be tremendous tension in these muscle groups below the level of our normal waking consciousness, but we are delving deeper to ascertain the state of those areas of our body that we normally ignore. Relax away that tension and move on to the thighs. Are you tensing them unnecessarily to keep yourself erect? Is there soreness or fatigue you had not noticed? Relax and observe their state and move on to the Gluteal muscles and again observe their current state and consciously relax them.

We do the same progressively through the abdomen and lower back, upper back and shoulder muscles, where so many of us store away the tension of our daily lives. Allow your shoulders to drop to their natural position instead of being pulled up to your ears. Our fight or flight mechanisms that worked so well in the case of physical threats have not yet evolved into a useful adaptation to the stresses of a boss and a job. These protective instincts tend to tighten up these muscle groups in an attempt to protect us, but it backfires and causes neck and back pain we carry through our lives. Let it go. You are safe and there is no threat here.

Relax and concentrate on the neck muscles and then those of the face. Release the mask you wear of the tough or weathered warrior and allow the tension to fade away. If you like you can now entertain a seed thought or visualize a safe and quiet place because you have now consciously released all of the pent up woes of your mind and emotions, which were stored in your physical organism.

This exercise may seem very basic to an experienced meditator, and it is a simple meditation, but it serves a number of purposes beyond the simple relaxed state it produces in the physical body. That in itself is a health promoting function and worthy of the time but it also trains us to focus our awareness in different areas of our physical bodies and become conscious of their state. This will become a larger part of future meditations when we are asked to focus on the energy centers within the etheric substructure rather than the physical organism itself. Focusing our attention in the Heart, Ajna or Crown center become an important part of the spiritual awakening that is enhanced and accelerated by the use of meditation. Visualizations become experiments in building with mental matter which, with effort and practice, can be brought to fruition on the physical plane.

THE MASTER IN THE HEART

This is a meditation taught by the Tibetan Master Djwahl Kuhl in the book Letters on Occult Meditation by Alice Bailey. I have simplified it somewhat so that it is easier for the beginning student. It may seem complex at first glance but once the general stages have been memorized and the explanations unnecessary, it is a fairly simple form.

There are many purposes served through the Master in the Heart meditation. The student is asked to do certain exercises while concentrating his attention in the Heart and Ajna (behind the brow) centers within his body.

Alignment:

The first stage is a centering of the consciousness and visualization of the threefold lower man coming into alignment with the higher self. The student is asked to see the lower self on rapport with, and as a channel for, expression of the Soul. This is done along with physical relaxation, the quieting of the mind and release of the sensory apparatus of the body. The sounding then of the sacred word, the OM, three times is done first quietly to stabilize and further quiet the mind, then more loudly to do the same for the emotional body and then even more loudly to work on the physical structure. The physical vibration of the sound against the roof of the mouth and throughout the body is intended to awaken the Ajna and heart centers into activity.

Affirmation:

The next stage is to proceed as if this blending and harmonizing process is complete. When we project ourselves into this future stage of alignment we hasten the process. As a man thinketh in his heart, so is he. The student is asked to repeat an affirmation. This is one I use every day at the close of my meditation.

I live in light and love
I am surrounded by beauty and abundance
I am expanding every day in every way

Visualization:

At this stage the student is asked to turn his attention to the etheric heart center. This is between the shoulder blades at the spine, not at the location of the physical Heart. Once this concentration is attained, he is to visualize a closed lotus bud. The lotus is used as a symbol of humanity for a number of reasons. It has its roots in the earth, the physical world, which is the first area of human consciousness. It grows through the waters, a symbol of the astral plane where man must grow through his emotional nature and overcome the tides of emotion in order to flower in consciousness in the Manasic plane. The flower blooms in the air above those waters. The lotus is, as man, complete though unexpressed in its seed form. All of the petals to come are present in the seed. They have simply not come to full expression as of yet.

The golden 12 pedaled lotus is visualized in the heart center. This is a visualization in the mind of the student of the existing, though unrealized flowering of the Egoic Lotus, the connection being forged with the causal body or Soul through this visualization. The bud is seen to expand and open in response to the sacred word as he repeats it silently. This is an expression of the will of the student to open the channel of communication and the response of the Soul seen in the opening of the heart. This energizes the heart center into greater activity. The petals of Love, Knowledge and Sacrifice open revealing the inner petals holding the jewel of Soul consciousness, pictured as an electric blue spark or flame, to be born within the cave of the human heart.

Within that jewel of cosmic fire the student is asked to build an image of himself with "The Master" in the heart. This master is his higher self. This is the God within. The first point of contact with the students own divinity. This is the Christ consciousness we will all come to know. The first place we will know God is within ourselves, as we are all an expression of divinity. As the student builds this image with loving attention, he is opening up to the conscious knowledge of his Soul's existence. As occultists we are form builders and we are simultaneously developing our ability to work with etheric, astral and manasic matter.

Meditation

The student is then asked to move his attention to the Ajna center behind the brow. This fosters and builds the natural connection between those two centers. His mind is prepared now for the concentration on a seed thought. All seed thoughts should have as their core, the fostering of communication of the lower self with the higher through self-forgetfulness, harmlessness and service. I have found this to be an extraordinarily powerful stage in the meditation.

A simple seed thought for this section of the meditation could be:

With self-forgetfulness I gather what I need for the helping of my fellow men.

The student is then asked to recite the Great Invocation. I have done this silently. This is the most overt act of service within the meditation itself. While the student is asked to contemplate the nature of service throughout other stages, and the work the student is accomplishing on him-self does constitute service, this is an outward expression more than inward work.

The Great Invocation

From the point of light within the mind of God Let light stream
forth into the minds of men Let Light descend on earth

From the point of love within the heart of God Let love stream forth
into the hearts of men May Christ return to Earth

From the center where the will of God is known
Let purpose guide the little wills of men
The purpose that the Masters know and serve

From the center which we call the race of men
Let the plan of love and light work out
And may it seal the door where evil dwells

Let light and love and power restore the plan on earth

The great invocation and its recitation goes outward to humanity to
help raise the group consciousness in a different way. This is a wish for
the raising of consciousness of all humanity. It is a wish that Love, Light,
and Power should stream forth into all of humanity. It anchors for the
student the fact of the divinity of all and that regardless of the work he
does for himself, the real work is for all.

This is culminated in the final affirmation in the meditation. The
student is asked to breathe forth, through the use of the sacred word,
(OM) energy into the New Group of World Servers. All of the power and
love he becomes capable of wielding through his personal development
is then put to use in strengthening the group and its effectiveness to
meet its goals. He is a repository and a conduit for loving energy and
strength which he now pours forth. The part (or unit) is put into the
service of the whole. As it becomes more powerful, more awake, and
more effective, it is of greater and greater use to the group which it seeks
to serve.

Simplified Outline:

Alignment:

Center the consciousness in the head and visualize the threefold lower man coming into alignment with the higher self.

The sounding then of the sacred word, the OM, three times is done first quietly to stabilize and further quiet the mind, then more loudly to do the same for the emotional body, and then even more loudly to work on the physical structure.

Affirmation:

I live in light and love
I am surrounded by beauty and abundance
I am expanding every day in every way

Visualization:

The golden 12 pedaled lotus is visualized in the heart center. The bud is seen to expand and open in response to the sacred word as he repeats it silently.

The petals of Love, Knowledge and Sacrifice open revealing the inner petals holding the jewel of Soul consciousness, pictured as an electric blue spark or flame, to be born within the cave of the human heart.

Within that jewel of cosmic fire the student is asked to build an image of himself with "The Master" in the heart.

Meditation

The student is then asked to move his attention to the Ajna center between the brows. This fosters and builds the natural connection between those two centers. His mind is prepared now for the concentration on the seed thought.

With self forgetfulness I gather what I need for the helping of my fellow men.

The Great Invocation

From the point of light within the mind of God Let light stream forth into the minds of men Let Light descend on earth

From the point of love within the heart of God Let love stream forth into the hearts of men May Christ return to earth

From the center where the will of God is known
Let purpose guide the little wills of men
The purpose that the Masters know and serve

From the center which we call the race of men
Let the plan of love and light work out
And may it seal the door where evil dwells

Let light and love and power restore the plan on earth
OM

We'd love to hear from you!

The collected works of Anthony J. Fisichella are available at Amazon.com

Rev. Douglas Fisichella

Email: ReverendDoug@SpiritualPracticality.com
Web: www.SpiritualPracticality.com
Blog: https://douglasfis.wordpress.com/
Twitter: @ReverandDoug
Facebook: www.facebook.com/ReverendDougF

BIBLIOGRAPHY

Helena Blavatsky –*The Secret Doctrine: Synthesis of Science, Religion and Philosophy Vol. III.* (London: The Theospohical Publishing Company, 1888)

Bruce Lipton – *The Biology of Belief: Unleashing the Power of Consciousness, Matter, & Miracles* (Hay House 2005)26

James Borg – *Body Language:7 Easy Lessons to Master the Silent Language (London: Pearson Education Ltd)*

Geoffery Hodson – *The Hidden Wisdom of The Holy Bible* (USA: Theosophical Publishing House 1993)

Andrew Cohen – *Evolutionary Enlightenment: A New Path to Spiritual Awakening* (New York: Select Books, 2011)

Terrence W. Deacon – *Incomplete Nature: How Mind Emerged From Matter* (New York: W.W. Norton & Company. 2011)

Bill Bryson – *A Short History of Nearly Everything* (USA: Broadway Books 2003)

Helena Blavatsky – *The Secret Doctrine: Synthesis of Science, Religion and Philosophy Vol. II.* (London: The Theospohical Publishing Company, 1888)

Helena Blavatsky – *The Secret Doctrine: Synthesis of Science, Religion and Philosophy Vol. I* (London: Theosophical Publishing Company 1888)

Natalie Banks – *The Golden Thread* (New York: Lucis Publishing Company 1963)

Arthur Koestler – *The Ghost in the Machine* (USA: Random House 1982)

Charles Darwin – *On the Origin of Species by means of Natural Selection* (London: John Murray Publishing 1859)

Stuart Edward White – *The Unobstructed Universe* (New York: E.P. Dutton and Company, Inc, 1940)

Brian Cox and Jeff Forshaw – *Why does E=mc2 (and Why Should we Care?)* (Philidelphia: De Capo Press 2009)

Anthony J. Fisichella *Echoes From Eternity* (USA: Authorhouse 2004)

Alice A Bailey – *A Treatise on Cosmic Fire* (New York: Lucis Publishing Company 1925)

Anthony Fisichella – *The Well of Wisdom* audio course on metaphysics. (Higher Ground Publishing 2004)

Richard Maurice Bucke – *Cosmic Consciousness: A Study in the Evolution of the Human Mind* (Detroit: Wayne State University Press, 1977)

William S. Burroughs – *The Soft Machine* (New York: Grove Press, 1961)

Alice A. Bailey – *The Light of the Soul"* (New York: Lucis Publishing Company, 1927)

Rhonda Byrne – *The Secret* (New York: Atria Books, 2006)

W. Timothy Gallwey - *The Inner Game of Tennis: The Classic Guide to the Mental Side of Peak Performance* (New York: Random House 1974)

Napoleon Hill – *Think and Grow Rich* (Cleveland, Ohio: The Ralston Publishing Co.1937)

Anthony J. Fisichella – *One Solitary Life – Book III: The Christ Epoch* (USA: Authorhouse 2008)

Alice A. Bailey – *A Treatise on Cosmic Fire* (New York: Lucis Publishing Company 1925)

Alice A. Bailey – *Discipleship in the New Age: Volume I* (New York: Lucis Publishing Company 1944)

Alice A. Bailey – *Discipleship in the New Age: Volume II* (New York: Lucis Publishing Company 1955)

Alice A. Bailey – *The Destiny of the Nations* (New York: Lucis Publishing Company 1949)

CPSIA information can be obtained
at www.ICGtesting.com
Printed in the USA
FSHW010514111219
64968FS